Inventing
Montana

Also by Ted Leeson

The Benchside Introduction to Fly Tying (with Jim Schollmeyer, 2006)

The Orvis Guide to Tackle Care and Repair (2006)

Tying Emergers (with Jim Schollmeyer, 2004)

Jerusalem Creek: Journeys into Driftless Country (2002)

Inshore Flies: Best Contemporary Patterns from the Atlantic and Gulf Coasts
(with Jim Schollmeyer, 2000)

Trout Flies of the East: Best Contemporary Patterns from East of the Rockies
(with Jim Schollmeyer, 1999)

Trout Flies of the West: Best Contemporary Patterns from the Rockies, West
(with Jim Schollmeyer, 1998)

The Fly Tier's Benchside Reference to Techniques and Dressing Styles (with
Jim Schollmeyer, 1998)

The Gift of Trout (editor, 1996)

The Habit of Rivers: Reflections on Trout Streams and Fly Fishing (1994)

Inventing
Montana

Dispatches from
the Madison Valley

Ted Leeson

Skyhorse Publishing

Skyhorse Publishing books may be purchased in bulk at special discounts for sales promotion, corporate gifts, fund-raising, or educational purposes. Special editions can also be created to specifications. For details, contact the Special Sales Department, Skyhorse Publishing, 555 Eighth Avenue, Suite 903, New York, NY 10018 or info@skyhorsepublishing.com.

www.skyhorsepublishing.com

10 9 8 7 6 5 4 3 2 1

Library of Congress Cataloging-in-Publication Data

Leeson, Ted.
Inventing Montana : dispatches from the Madison Valley / Ted Leeson.
p. cm.
ISBN 978-1-60239-796-5 (alk. paper)
1. Fishing--Montana--Anecdotes. 2. Montana--Description and travel. I. Title.
SH517.L44 2009
978.6--dc22
2009012165

Printed in the United States of America

For Liz, who asked

CONTENTS

I wish they would not call me a hedonist; it gives such a wrong impression to those who do not know Greek.

—Walter Pater

Preface

MONTANA IS NOT A PLACE. IT IS MERELY THE NAME OF A PLACE, A CONvenience of language, ambiguously significant. Montana does not even comprise a distinct physiographic region; it specifies only an arbitrary geopolitical construct of the type always betrayed by straight borders on a map, drawn by diplomacy or war. Even the Rocky Mountains from which it takes its name occupy just a part of it, and the lesser portion at that, though to me, they define where Montana begins—in an arc of stony vertebrae on the long spine of the Americas, in the ribs of rock and veins of rivers, in a skin of soil and the pulse of seasons. What is called "Montana" arises in part from our exchanges with this living space, one organism to another. Without such transactions, there is a geography, but not a place.

Place is a human invention, a negotiated space lying somewhere between the fact of the land and our desire to inhabit it. It exists as both a discovery and a creation, a cartographer's scrawl and coordinates on a map of the imagination. The West has always been this way, a history of invention that reaches back to a time when the American frontier lay on the shores of Massachusetts, Virginia, Florida. Long before it became a physical reality for the first immigrants, the West represented an idea—a deliverance from evil, conjectures of El Dorado, a reprieve from the past, a roll of the dice, the lure of a new beginning, the garden of Eden, the haunt of savages, the great untried, a flight to and a flight from—an immense silence that echoed back every dream and nightmare whispered into it. And in the intervening four centuries, it has proved both a redemption realized and a misconceived *a priori* desire into which the realities of the landscape and its people were often unremittingly coerced. And so there is a Montana of Yellowstone and Glacier country that gives refuge to nature and spirit and another that's home to an open-pit mine deeper than Lake Superior, a raw wound that still weeps its toxins. Countless other versions lie in between, for every place is as much created as it is found.

An acquaintance of mine, a professional photographer, some years back left his home in eastern Europe and made his way across the United States. He eventually stopped on the banks of the Gallatin River, where he fashioned for himself a place in the landscape that he discovered. I have never met a man so thoroughly smitten with a sense of the lucky intersection of his life and location. For him, Montana is the light that floods his lens. It is also elk—he photographs them, hunts them, and sometimes hikes the mountains simply to watch them—and the deer that bed in his riverbottom land, and the gregarious pack of Jack Russell terriers that weaves around him when he walks and upon which he dotes unapologetically. Before he became a father, he told me that he wanted to name his firstborn "Montana," after the place that he had made and that made him, a perpetuation linked to the land. When I suggested that it was a rather unusual given name for an American child, he said, "Yes, I know this."

Other friends and people I've met—fishing guides, writers, shopkeepers, bartenders, seasonal migrants like myself, ranchers, nine-to-fivers, those who were born here and those who chose to come—have fashioned their own versions of Montana, composing their circumstances of living in ways that are mindfully aligned with the life of the land and rivers. Certain people, of course, will undertake this kind of mutuality anywhere they discover a landscape that communicates directly with the heart. But it seems somehow more possible here, amid these spaces and their immense interiors. Montana is said to be rich in natural resources, which I take to mean the raw materials from which we create place.

This book contains, in a sense, my own Montana, which began taking shape over two decades ago when I spent a brief few days here. They came almost as an afterthought, at the end of a weeks'-long pilgrimage to the trout-fishing shrines of the West, the kind of expedition most fly anglers make at least once in their lives, partly because it gives one's fishing identity a certain credibility, and partly because it would be a shame to die without having a look at some of the loveliest rivers on the continent. Five of us made the trip, a digressive excursion that took us, among other places, to spring creeks in southern Idaho, both forks of the Snake River, the waters around Jackson Hole, and on up into Yellowstone country where the transmission in my pickup truck, already fearful of steep grades, responded to the terrors of unprecedented inclines by grinding itself expensively into shiny steel chips. The work was remarkably thorough, and we were towed the fifty-six miles from Fishing Bridge to a West Yellowstone garage and there awaited a rebuild from Bozeman. A three-day eternity later, we left to recuperate on the banks of the nearest trout stream, which turned out to be the Madison River, water I knew only by reputation.

Southwest Montana arguably contains the country's highest density of first-rate trout water; the region is to fly fishing what the Golden Crescent is to opium production, and does a similarly brisk business. The Madison flows through the heart of it, a river with as distinctive a stream signature as any I have seen. It runs shallow for its breadth over a cobbled bed of water-rounded stones, clear and light, a glittering chop of water in endless motion; it has been called the Forty-mile Riffle, which is not entirely accurate, but close. All trout water evokes hope, but no other river I know of summons it in quite the same way. Every rock and boulder on the bottom, from bank to bank, looks as though it must conceal a trout in the shelter of current behind it or beneath the soft pillow of water in front. You cannot cast a fly anywhere in the river without the conviction that it's drifting over fish. That you may know better counts for nothing in the overpowering impression of possibility, one of the pleasant illusions from which an angling life is built. The Madison is a river of immense persuasive capacities.

I no longer recall how many trout I caught in the couple of days we stayed—one, maybe two—but that was enough. Sufficiency on a trout stream comes in many forms, and for three weeks or a month each summer over the past twenty years, I have been returning, always in the company of friends; some of them come out annually, others now and then as life allows, and a couple of them were part of that first trip and discovered the place as I did. We headquarter each season at the same house, affordably rented since even collectively we do not constitute a person of means. It sits on the first of a succession of benchlike landforms that recede in ascending tiers from the river, surrounded by range land, framed by the Madison Range to the east and the Gravelly Range to the west, with an open and dramatic prospect of the valley between. To the essentials that the place provides—an engaging setting both spacious and private, modest but comfortable quarters, and above all else a trout stream at hand—we add those ingredients that are commonly found among longtime friends and make such affairs seem unique to the people involved and rather ordinary to everyone else. In the end, the house contains much good company and good humor, interesting conversation, a 64-quart marine cooler refreshed daily with beer and ice, and an abundance of recreational cooks enthusiastically undeterred by their own extreme amateurism. After our fashion, we make the best of all this.

These gatherings focused first on fishing in the ferociously single-minded way of younger people, who generally cannot get enough of anything. Trout still remain resolutely at the center of it, but less exclusively so now. The fact of familiar return, both actual and anticipated, has altered the nature of things. It's difficult to pinpoint how or when repetition turns into habit, habit to custom, custom to tradition, and tradition into ritual. But given the right soil, proper growing conditions, and some luck, the first will become the last, which is both more intimate and more expansive, and casts everything in a different light, including the fishing. Even small rituals serve to enlarge, rather than duplicate, experience. Repetition provides the mechanism, but the function is continuity and extension, the enactment of something ongoing, like the making of a story. For me, Montana is a work in progress.

A few weeks a year, even for two decades, does not add up to any great length of time, and I could hardly claim to know Montana beyond the tiny fraction of it I periodically inhabit. What roots I have here, if they can be said to exist at all, run no deeper than those of a potted plant. And in one respect, my time here is an artificially cultivated experience that might be tempting to dismiss as a strain of self-delusive tourism, like the Wall Street hedge-fund viper who spends ten days a year in a rented slip at Marblehead, living aboard a B40 he doesn't own and can't sail, capering about the deck in a commodore's hat and thinking himself quite the sailor. To fall into this category, even inadvertently, is my worst fear.

But I do not feel myself a tourist, a person to whom only the scenery happens. I don't come to visit Montana. I come here to live. And if my familiarity with the place runs only skin-deep, I am satisfied, for it is our skins that wrap us in sensation, register heat and cold, contact and pressure.

It is the skin that tingles with pleasure and skin that raises the hair on your arm or the back of your neck. The eardrum is but specialized skin, and even vision, it has been suggested, originated in the dermal cells, where sight evolved from touch. My knowledge of the landscape and rivers may extend no farther than what I can gather through my own senses, but to go skin-deep is not as trivial as it seems. I get a little suspicious of people who assure me that they "know the place," though I suppose a few of them genuinely do. Mostly, I think, they mean that they know their way around it, which is rather different, though still something. I cannot make even that claim. I lose myself easily here; it is one of the reasons I come.

The Montana of my experience is in some respects large, as it must be in a place that urges upon you the overwhelming fact of physical space. For the most part, however, its dimensions are modest and local. I come here most often in the limited way of a fisherman, more apt to take notice of some things than others, but always trusting that the best places offer many conduits to discovery and, like the best rivers, are characterized in part by their capacity for surprise. Our stay here spans a few weeks somewhere between the Fourth of July and the end of August, and geographically, it remains confined largely to the Madison River Valley, and even then only part of it, that length of river between Quake Lake and Beartrap Canyon. We sometimes venture beyond these boundaries and might do so more often if we could come up with a good enough reason for it. But if you let it, the shape of locality, whatever its size, molds the contours of experience, and like the valley, the time lived here takes form from a convergence of tributaries: of friends who trickle in from distant parts, of talk and ideas, of unexpected discovery, of impressions and perceptions, of days on the river, of the river itself and the land that creates it. What already exists here and what is brought to it meet in the profoundly fortunate confluence of place. Here, as William Kittredge says, "I feel most securely connected to luck."

What I call "Montana" is a kind of shorthand for all of these things, a metaphor of sorts—or more precisely, a metonym, that figure of speech in which we name the container to stand for what it contains. We say "the kettle is boiling," when we actually mean the water, or that "The White House announced," when in fact a cabal of unnamed insiders spun some twaddle and extruded it through the official spokeshole. It is a peculiar trope, useful beyond the manufacture of bureaucratic anonymity, and sometimes necessary. Metonym trades away literal accuracy for a different kind of truthfulness. We give to things the name of the enclosure that holds them all because we do not experience the parts discretely but inseparably and because the parts themselves are sometimes inexpressible on their own. The names of all our important places become metonymical; it is one of the ways we contain their importances in words. A figure of speech gathers them together under one roof, into the same proximity that we feel in the living of them.

Montana is a word that closes distances, a name for a curved roof of sky and a place fashioned beneath it.

Corvallis, Oregon
March 2009

Inventing
Montana

1

INVENTING MONTANA

Beneath the aquamarine of a high-summer sky, beyond the rising ripples of earth-warmed air, under the deckled shade of cottonwoods in the deep of an August afternoon, we have deployed ourselves in the various postures of voluptuary indolence.

The Writer reclines in a derelict aluminum lounge chair, a glass of wine in one hand and a field guide to birds spread open on her lap. Pinned to the brim of her overscaled straw visor is the stylized coil of a hammered-silver rattlesnake, about which you are left to draw your own conclusions. Early in life, she played the accordion and should still be considered dangerous. Next to her, the Painter sits with a block of cold-press paper propped on the knee of her crossed leg and squints through sunglasses, first at the Madison Range, ten miles distant, and then at a metal tray of watercolors beside her. The ochre and lavender forms of a mountainscape take shape on the page. Their talk wanders freely between owls and pigments, the Writer wondering whether tinted lenses distort colors in the landscape and on the palette. "Probably," the Painter admits. "But it's not the mountains anyway, just a picture in my head."

Nearby, slumped down in a camp chair with his elbows propped on the armrests to steady an enormous pair of binoculars, the Photographer studies the open rangeland beyond the trees, in perpetual thrall to a world revealed through curved glass. He has just driven over from the Bighorn River and gives an account of the fishing, never once lowering the glasses as he watches an osprey carve spirals into the luminous afternoon. "There were lots of people," he keeps saying, "but the fish are nice." Up on the wooden porch behind him, the Mechanic reassembles and tunes an expensive bicycle dismantled for transport, slowly spinning the rear wheel and listening attentively as it clicks like a locust in the sun. Something suspect, inaudible to the rest of us, catches his ear, and instantly he falls upon it with tools; the thought of imperfection in physical systems is intolerable to him.

The Cook, rangy-limbed and knob-jointed, sits at one end of a picnic bench and leans against the redwood table. The half-smoked Honduran maduro in his hand has gone cold, and an inch of fine ash cantilevers uncertainly above his beer glass. He is listening to the Hindu, who, with a shaved head and wire spectacles, bears an uncanny resemblance to the young Gandhi. The faint inflections of British East India and the idioms of Valley-speak shape the edges of his speech as he talks of growing up around Bombay and Los Angeles. Between them sits a half-empty bowl of Flathead cherries, a smaller one of pits and stems, the crisp shards of grilled lentil-flour flatbreads, and a bowl of herb chutney finished with sizzling black mustard seed. A wooden cutting board close by holds the remains of a dense Genoese sausage cured to the color of amaranth and half a slab of smoked steelhead from Oregon. Strewn elsewhere about the table are olives from Greece, farmstead cheeses from Bulgaria and England, a peppery Hungarian *ajvar*, a baguette still smelling of warm yeast baked by the Writer an hour ago. Cuttings of wild mustard and foxtail barley sprout from the emerald neck of an empty magnum of champagne that has marked our return. Other bottles stand here and there in various phases of dispatch. Stained napkins ruffle in a faint wind. The food has not been orchestrated in accordance with any higher-order gastronomic harmony but, rather, like a personal library, assembled with the quirky logic of what pleases.

"I don't ask for much," the Cook interrupts, "but what I get should be of high quality."

"Dude, this is so un-American," the Hindu observes, his small gold earring winking in the light.

Sitting on the wooden porch steps, I labor to rebuild a trashed leader, an operation that is taking longer than the average kidney transplant, and dip each blood knot in a glass of India pale ale to lubricate it for tightening. Behind me, rigged fly rods slouch against the house, and beyond them, several pairs of chest waders wilt over a wood-rail fence in poses of limp exhaustion, like sailors returned from shore leave. We have fished away our first morning and part of the afternoon casting big attractor dry flies, those controlled detonations of deer hair and hackle that bespeak a light-headed optimism and the glad hearts of those who have time to burn. In a minor form of ritual, every year begins with hurling these toilet brushes as a form of reconnaissance, a way of taking the temperature of the trout by seeing how gamely they might rise to these monstrous improbabilities and so gauge how exacting or undemanding the fishing might be this summer. Like most anglers, we tend to the easy money first, just in case. That it has failed to pan out today troubles no one yet.

Those of us who fish—which is nearly everyone—split up earlier in the day as we ordinarily do, some to float, others to wade. I went with the Painter, who is also my wife, to a favored reach of water a few miles from the town of Ennis. In this stretch of river, the Madison divides into scores of little channels around scores of little islands, sculpting a riverscape of small streams wandering through miles of a mazelike archipelago that is everything an angler on foot could hope for. Around every island flows a miniature trout stream, and roaming about, you might fish a few dozen of them in a day, each one drawing you farther on than the last. It is not really possible to get lost among them, but you don't always know exactly where you are, which accounts in part for why I like coming here. As the paths of water multiply, the river broadens and shallows, and the streambed becomes more tractable. Each season, winter ice and the high waters of spring rearrange the cobbles and gravel, usually in small ways, though over the years you might see the accumulated reconfigurings completely dry up old channels and cut new ones, watch shoals rise and become islands, and islands wear away to riffles as the river slowly revises the story of itself and remakes its own profoundly inviting version of Montana.

Coming back to this water courts the perils of all revisitation, among them a temptation to nostalgia and delusional expectations. The workings of memory are less apt to acknowledge themselves as corruptive than to suspect that someone has rearranged the furniture in their absence, though I suppose both produce their discrepancies. Then, too, you face the usual disorientations that attend any renewed acquaintanceship; there are bearings to be taken, landmarks reestablished, and much to catch up on. The Painter and I have come for the fishing but also out of a sense of informal proprietorship, that secondary form of possession that represents somewhat more than a feeling of simple fondness and somewhat less than one of explicit superintendence—an impulse commonly shared by those who incline to the tropisms of place. Beyond taking stock of the trout, we wish to see how the river and landscape have fared more generally, which, as in most places these days, turns out to be both better and worse than expected.

The Painter's favorite water—a slow cutbank pool at the tail of an island—appears to have weathered the winter handsomely. The soft soil of the bank, always at risk of collapse, has held; the incoming channel has gained volume since last year, freshening the current and excavating a broader and deeper basin. Some distance downstream, on the other hand, still more of the riverbank has been hogged away for yet another prefab mansionette complete with streamside septic and the usual apocalyptic admonitions against trespassing. Not far away, a gravel road has been paved, and in the distance, another building or two has appeared on a once-unbroken vista to the mountains. Like us, the place has changed as it has grown older and, like us, looked in rather better shape when it was young; but on the whole, we cannot complain about either. Whatever cause might be found for regret or discontent is superseded by the exhilaration of finding ourselves here once more, regardless of condition.

To arrive at a place and remember it is one thing; to retrieve a sense of one's own presence in that place is quite another and goes beyond the validation or amendment of specific recollections—the way a landscape looks and sounds and behaves—and goes beyond even reexperiencing those details as familiar. The recovery of that former presence comes instead as a kind of full-body recognition, both supersensory and subconscious; everything about the place comes flooding in and is admitted directly through the skin as a feeling of knowing. The Painter and I walk among the channels, reabsorbing the landscape, gauging its alterations and persistences in a way that always attends such returns. An important part of this inventory is conducted with a fly rod, and almost everywhere we find smaller fish, a predictable outcome in this water yet a fact I somehow manage to forget every year. But they are trout all the same, and consequently wonderful, and they do signify the promise of future summers. So one is quite pleased to find them in abundance, if somewhat less so to catch them that way.

We eventually make our way to the Painter's cutbank pool, still flinging the ridiculous dust bunnies we've fished all day. The spring runoff, however, has apparently brought with it a winter-killed deer and beached the vigorously decomposing carcass on a dry shoal not thirty yards directly upwind of us—a bearable cross if the pool fishes well, but a compelling deterrent otherwise. Today proves otherwise, and we decide to leave, having obtained at least part of what we came for: the first foretaste of a month's worth of tomorrows and with them the luxury, should it become necessary, of having time to wait until the fishing picks up.

Back at the house, we find a comfortable spot to sit under the trees. The others straggle in at intervals and join us in the shade of the cottonwoods, a natural space of conversation, concourse, and refreshment that serves variously as our café alfresco, roundtable, lecture hall, and front-row seat at the performances of sunlight and shadow. It is our School of Athens, our sitting room at the Sportsman's Club, and a crucible for fusing our collective eccentricities into a reasonably benign form of communal anarchy. Today, we have all fished water long familiar to the rest and make the usual inquiries about particular spots, traffic on the river, and fly patterns, and trade opinions on the prospects in general, how this year will stack up against past ones. A single morning's fishing, of course, and especially the first one, does not reveal a great deal about the big picture, though this kind of obstacle doesn't stop anglers from speculating; we require very little in the way of raw material. Over a sufficient length of time, however, the big picture always looks about the same, as do the conclusions we draw about it—the river will fish well some days and not others, a point beyond dispute but one that leaves unanswered important questions about which days will be which and in what proportion. This pretty much exhausts the subject, and the talk turns to other matters. Books, paints, and field glasses appear, and we settle into the deep cushion of the afternoon.

We are also waiting, not with impatience but industriously engaged in what the little men in Human Resources would uncomprehendingly call "doing nothing."

RUN, RABBIT, RUN

Of all the animals, only Man has to remind himself that he possesses life.

—Marvin Bell

Any enterprise centered on angling automatically forfeits any pretense to seriousness in the ordinary world. I wouldn't call this the whole point of fishing, just part of it. Aside from the fish, who undoubtedly have their own opinion on the matter, and regardless of whatever it may have been in the more distant past, fishing is now at heart a form of play. I have always assumed this much to be obvious, but judging from the current trajectory of the sport, evidently it is not. Modern angling is uncomfortable with the idea and prefers to regard itself more along the lines of modern medicine, as an acutely specialized body of knowledge dispensed by a priesthood of experts. It tends to operate in the oxygen-depleted atmosphere of high gravitas or, more recently, in the overstimulated public displays of cultivated fanaticism. Those deficient in the requisite intensity—who fail to mount a sufficiently strategic angling campaign, do not whoop in ecstatic wargasm as the battle rages or pump the air with a victory fist at the climactic moment of conquest —are left to marinate in the unpleasant secretions of their own inadequacy. The naïf who concedes that he cannot translate into deadly tactics the squirming mysteries on the underside of a river rock, cannot crack the existential conundrum of the masking hatch or double-haul into his backing exposes only the discomfiting spectacle of his own small and hairless glands. Among experts, such people evoke a complex kind of pity.

One might hope that the larger world, sensibly insulated from the interior antics of the sport, would furnish a corrective of sorts, since the nonangler more readily grasps the nature of fishing as play. But for the most part, the larger world is in no position to gallop to anyone's aid in the matter. In the prevailing social climate, play is either dismissed as the pointless frivolity of kittens and uselessly small children or enlisted as a sinister pretext for the acquisition of marketable skills. A briskly successful child-enrichment industry pumps out "toys" that covertly teach Mandarin, differential equations, and the principal exports of Chad, exhorting the users to have "fun" as it slips an instructional mickey into their sippy cups. Along similar lines, the fairly recent and massive outbreak of organized sports for the young, disengaged at last from the foolishly quaint notion that "everybody gets to play," teaches sacrifice to the cause, persevering through the pain, the grimmer facts of the food chain, the sanctity of competition, and the holiness of winning, along with other aids to abet a worker bee soon to be toiling in the now-global hive. After time expires, outraged parents file suit against the coach or pistol-whip a referee, impromptu seminars in the techniques of American conflict resolution. This same attitude toward the business of fun has spawned one of the more frightening coinages to come out of the minivan scare, the "playdate," in which, as I understand it, my children's people contact your children's people to negotiate a form of social transaction that might have been drawn up by some sharpshooter in Mergers & Acquisitions. I imagine this is supposed to sound more grown-up and to disguise in wishful sophistication the fact that little girls delight chiefly in bossing one another around and little boys simply want to blow things up. But modern American parenting discourages these honorable occupations and instead straps its offspring to a cheerless rocket ship bound for precocious adulthood. All of this presumably aims at preparing them for the business of making a living, which, increasingly it seems, has become identified with living itself.

Not that we let ourselves off the hook. We hold notions of our own play to the same low standards and view our own leisure in a similarly utilitarian way, that is, through the portal of work—partly as an escape from it and partly as preparation for it. We "recharge the battery," as the expression goes, so that we might return to work at full power and insert our prongs back into the grid of the great American cash machine. Either way, play is construed in terms subordinate to making a living. The system, unsurprisingly, advocates this viewpoint, though with its usual psychotropic logic. The Mechanic, who works at a large and well-known high-tech manufacturing facility, recently told me of a co-worker who sacrificed his free time and burned the midnight and weekend oils in the way of so many contemporary middle managers struggling to keep their jobs. This behavior was duly noted in his annual personnel review with the caution that he was taking insufficient vacation time, the lack of which could cause his performance to drop below current levels. He was to consider himself warned. I'm not certain who should get credit here, Orwell or Kafka, but the gist of it comes through in spite of itself: leisure is to be encouraged insofar as it promotes greater efficiency, higher output, more durable service. Spend too much time at play, though, and you become a power drain and a figure of suspiciously skewed priorities. Americans envision their leisure in the same way that, as Jim Harrison has pointed out, they envision their food—"as mere fuel for the realities." We play in order to work; the sweat of one's brow is the natural state of man, the wages of the original sin of being human. I recall being told that the system was set up this way—something about sitting around naked and eating apples, though I could be misremembering. I never understood it very clearly.

Possibly, our attitudes toward work and play have come down to us as a national inheritance. They may represent, as H. L. Mencken claimed, a sort of reverse historical hangover, the lingering aftereffects of the chronic underindulgences of Puritanism, which looked upon leisure with deep theological misgivings and equated idleness with perdition. At the least, we do appear to harbor a mistrust or guilt about play that compels us to camouflage it as something else, to align it with something more respectable than the devil's workshop. And so we have, it seems, professionalized our leisure to make it more consistent with the values of professional life—industry, competition, risk, penalties, and payoffs—as a way of legitimizing play, which I suppose means we have Puritanized our leisure. In my lifetime, this tendency has been allied, not coincidentally, with the extreme commoditization of sports in general, from the pros on down to the tenderest ranks of amateurs. The line between sport, which is ritualized play, and sports, which is ritualized business (or ritualized war as William James would have it—same thing, really) has become disturbingly blurred.

Fishing has hardly escaped this fate; if anything, the sport has rushed toward it, casting arms outstretched to embrace the boggling idea of angling tournaments, which, when you peel away the hype, are in essence a form of commercial fishing. Casting for cash and glory has grown significantly popular, not merely among participants but, even stranger still, among television spectators. Armchair angling has become a business and, judging by the rodentlike proliferation of such events, a paying one. The format and media coverage of these spectacles show an amalgam of elements from the PGA Tour, professional automobile racing, and TV game shows, with all the indispensables of the contemporary American sporting event: celebrity superstars upholstered in product logos, underdogs and frontrunners, the rivalries and manufactured drama, the cheesy pageantry, the Moment of Truth, a hefty paycheck (which hit seven figures a while back), the postgame clichés, advertising revenue, and endorsements. I recently watched one of these broadcasts, a top-money competition from which would emerge the bass-fishing potentate of the known universe. From a studio wallpapered in television monitors, a play-by-play man narrated the action, darting from one remote feed to another, filling the backstory with edited tape clips of the competitors, who did not appear to be "fishing" so much as derricking points into the live well of a glittering ruby-flake spacecraft. The fish that survived would later go free, having played their part in what amounts to little more than a corporately sponsored form of paintball. At one point, in a seizure of admiration for the contestants, the TV host bestowed on them that most sacred of American encomiums: "These aren't just fishermen—they're athletes." This might have been true, though you couldn't tell by looking. But the point is that to be merely fishing hints at the need for explanation or apology; to participate in an athletic contest— the winners, the prizes, the statistics—that's something we all understand. Everyone's behind that.

Even fly fishing has been sucked into the accelerating gloom, with the growth of casting competitions and certification regimens, fly-tying contests, and, most recently, angling tournaments of its own, a few of them international in scope. Some of these sprouted from relatively humble roots, the Jackson Hole One Fly Event, for instance; though, to be sure, some anglers caught a whiff of doom even here and opposed this kind of thing from the start. Compared to warm-water competitions, which have extended to nearly every species with fins, fly-fishing tournaments scarcely register on the radar, and many of them, perhaps most, take place on an unthreatening and ignorable scale. Still, some of them are already appearing on television, and if the coverage looks crude compared to the largemouth sweepstakes, that will change. To dismiss these things as small potatoes is to disregard the cautionary tale of the professional bass circuit.

Viewed from a sufficient distance, the whole notion of fishing contests does have its comic aspects; up close I find it disheartening. Perhaps my reaction only reflects a distaste for this sort of competition in particular and for institutionalized fun in general. Despite how it seems, I am not so much objecting to the tournaments themselves (at least here) as to the attitudes they represent, certainly about fishing but indirectly about our notions of leisure and recreation. We appear determined to sanction or dignify play by formalizing it, infusing it with the principles of the marketplace, and bringing to it the same kinds of metrics that infest nearly every other aspect of life, from the rubrics that measure job performance to the data-collection software that monitors your Internet clicks. Our recreation now runs on the same rails as business. We plan our free time like a day at the office; a weekend spent at home is one in which we can "get a few things done." We no longer simply wish to enjoy our leisure; we wish to be successful at it.

Maybe there's no great harm in all of this, but I don't think we need to exhume the corpse of Thoreau—or Rousseau or even Marx—to see that there's no great virtue in it either. In my lifetime there has been a telling mutation in the terminology applied to the products of technology. When I was growing up, people referred to them as "time-saving" or "labor-saving" devices, with the implication that they could put a little bit of your life back into your own pocket. Now they are almost universally and uncritically known as "productivity tools," with the assumption that any time or labor saved gets reinvested in producing even more—of whatever. It doesn't matter. It's pretty much all the same. The preliminary results for the twenty-first century have just come in, and they offer little consolation; more of us work more—harder and longer, with less time to ourselves and diminishing satisfaction. The expanding space that livelihood occupies in our lives, and so in our leisure, is what crosses my mind when I hear the phrase "identity theft."

But play need not be either an adjunct to work or its mirror image. The word suggests other possibilities—the looseness or latitude in a mechanical assembly, for instance, like the play in a steering wheel. It describes that certain window of liberty that goes unnoticed by the linkages of the larger system, a kind of indeterminacy or independence that is eliminated in the truly precise machine, where any specific input has an equally specific and predictable output. To be deprived of play involves a kind of inevitability or fatedness; to possess it signifies a little room to move without detection or reprisal, a kind of free space that can be physical but also imaginative. This kind of play occurs beyond the ordinary and differs from a simple absence of labor. Neither work nor its opposite, it defines some third space fashioned between them but apart from both, where the only imperative is attending to the impulses of curiosity, thought, and inclination.

Play is not effortless or the same as idleness, though it sometimes requires being idle, and to play is emphatically not "to do nothing." What play is to do, however, is one of the objects of play to discover.

"CONSIDER THE LILIES . . ."

how they grow; they toil not, neither do they spin. And yet I say unto you that even Solomon in all his glory was not arrayed like one of these.

—Matthew 6:28–29

One of the virtues of what was once called "removing to the country" is that when you get there, you're in the country, at least if you've done it right. And Montana furnishes some spectacular country to remove to; its natural beauties both subtle and sublime have been articulated, if not always captured, in words and images for at least as long as Montana has officially existed. It produces above all the impression of overwhelming spaciousness, immensities of landscape and great sweeps of sky that at first and perhaps inevitably one encounters as something detached, a scenic backdrop of sorts, as though you're looking through the window of a car even when you're not. It invites a kind of touristic appreciation that, while not illegitimate, does decline with growing familiarity in the way of most novelties. Over time, it gives way to the experience of scale, which is rather different from simply seeing something big. It induces an almost synesthetic reaction, a feeling of distances receding from you, a physical sensation of space, perhaps similar in its mechanism to the way height registers on an acrophobic, but infinitely preferable in its effects. Eventually, you come to regard the landscape, its austerities and extravagances, from the inside looking out rather than the reverse. And the view, to my taste, improves considerably.

The house to which we return every year stands in the seclusion of trees on a long, flat expanse of benchland that slopes to the river on one side and climbs to the next bench on the other, like the level tread of a stair between two sloping risers. It is not an altogether domesticated setting, certainly far less so than the rural agricultural land of my Midwestern childhood that we simply called "farm country." There, despite the sometimes long distances between farmsteads, the fields and woodlots and livestock were long settled in and quite at home, fixtures of the landscape. Here on the bench, some of the land is under cultivation but most remains simply range, and cattle graze as temporary squatters rather than residents. On the intermontane sage and grass steppes, even small-scale ranchers require a fair amount of this semi-arid land to make a living. Most have significantly more than the minimum, and so the ranches remain far apart. More people have arrived here with the passing years, as they have everywhere, the conspicuously wealthy choosing conspicuous sites, while the more modest summer-house and retirement crowds have consolidated into enclaves of rural suburbia mostly hidden from sight. But on the whole and compared to most places, this one contains relatively few people. Our closest neighbor lives about half a mile away, the next nearest almost twice that, and our particular location has about it a comfortable atmosphere of removal.

At the same time, you would not mistake this spot for wilderness, though on a clear day and with a little elevation, you can see some from here—or what resembles wilderness, or at least passes for it in the Lower 48. The term lacks any real precision. At the least, and without elevation, you can observe not far away expanses of essentially uninhabited backcountry that might safely be called wild. Wilderness is a collective concept, but wild an individual one, and if we do not live in the former, the latter surrounds us as it filters in and passes through or shares the territory permanently. The cottonwoods out back and the great horned owl that hunts from them; the lupine and blanketflower; the black bear and twin cubs that wandered past the house one afternoon, pawing at anthills; the orphaned cub that has returned for the last two autumns and left pawprints on the storm door; the mountain bluebirds, sandhill cranes, and meadowlarks; the trout in the river—none of these know themselves as anything but wild. Neither do the foxes and kits that denned for a few seasons under the machine shed and on the hillside out front, or the purple gentian, or the mice in the kitchen, or the wolverine we twice saw shuffling across the road to polish off an antelope carcass. They will show you all the instincts of wildness, as will even the speckled *Callibaetis* that sometimes land on the window screens, for even a mayfly possesses a wild thing's heart and sense of the world. And if the antelope and deer act more at home here, their snuffling through the grass around the house denotes only a convenient habituation; to them, we represent a form of mobile shrubbery, nothing more than part of the scenery as they go about their animal business.

The natural world that thrives outside our door, or on the benches or bottomland or in the river, holds a continual and enduring interest, and like a great many people, we take pleasure in simply watching it. Most of us have made a lifelong habit of such observation, though in varying degrees of formality. The Writer explores natural history subjects. The Photographer specializes in images of aquatic insects. The Painter has taught herself botany in the best and literal tradition of the amateur—that is, "one who loves" a chosen pursuit. The Mechanic has a fascination with the clockwork of the night sky. One of us knows a bit of geology and sometimes heads out to find rocks or fossils. Birds are a universal favorite. None of us could lay the remotest claim to expertise in such matters, and so each year we arrive with a small dump truck's worth of field guides to every conceivable kind of creature, phenomenon, system, and manifestation of nature—except for, perhaps, tropical coral reefs, though we might even have one or two of these. Bill and Betsy Segal, who rent us the place, have a bookshelf or two stocked with others. We rarely step outside the house without binoculars, which in this landscape of distances count for much. We spend some part, often the greater one, of every day casually or intently occupied with the world out-of-doors, enjoying its variety and beauty. "Beautiful," in fact, is the word most people would use to describe it.

But when we appreciate this beauty, I wonder what we are really responding to; or, rather, I wonder about the nature of our responses, whether evoked by the mountainscape that forms our eastern horizon or by the goldenrod spider with a lavender lightning bolt down each side of its ivory abdomen that lives in a purple clover blossom out back. Certainly forms intrigue us—the angles of tectonic ridges, the anatomical swells and curves of the benchland, the broccoli shapes of cottonwoods, the crescent of current around a river rock—as do compositions of forms that appeal or surprise. We appreciate texture in the fernlike ruff at a heron's throat and the silky skin of a trout. The emerald iridescence of a hummingbird, the scarlet-orange of Indian paintbrush, and a thousand other colors and combinations of them in the landscape please us. We admire the liquid glide of pelicans and the precision of nighthawks and the intricate phrasing of bird song.

That is to say, nature elicits from us an essentially aesthetic response—an authentic appreciation, unquestionably, but also one that involves a detachment of sorts. We engage the natural world scenically, even cinematically, and end up valuing many of the same qualities we value in art; people often summon the word "picturesque." This form of engagement discovers, because it seeks, a pleasingness of impressions; it can look at the decaying remains of a white-tailed deer and see beauty in the vault of ribs or the smooth bone hollow of an eye socket. Even in these things we find a felicitousness, a well-chosenness, a kind of perfection. Such an appreciation is passionate, complex, and true, but also one that perhaps answers more to the attributes of the natural world than to what those attributes signify, what they are attributes of, which is the natural order itself. And I am wondering how we reconcile what we see in nature with what we know about it.

For the natural world, like the human one, generally shapes up as a pretty hard business, and for many of the same reasons, chief among them the relentlessness of making a living. Everything in nature behaves with purpose and direction, and what may look to us like leisure, or even play among the young, furthers the husbanding of energy or the acquisition of survival skills. And what appears to us as beauty—indeed, is beauty—is also something else. We see the doe and fawn that bound away at our approach as the incarnation of wild grace; in their own minds, they are fleeing for their lives. The red-tailed hawk that soars the afternoon sky like our own dreams of flying is bent on killing lunch. Part of the year, bird song serves the grave business of sex; much of the rest of the time, it talks trash to territorial interlopers. The riot of blooms in an alpine meadow, their premeditated architectures and calculated fragrances, the shape of leaves and spread of roots—all represent a desperate cry for the kind of attention on which their lives depend: suitors, water, sun, and space. What seems a glorious raiment is in fact a survival suit.

We not only know all of this but regard it, too, as beautiful, intensely fascinating and absorbing. We are not blind to the million murders a minute that take place in nature, but when we observe one, we consider it highly interesting—or, in the case of rising trout, quite wonderful. Confronting a natural world awash in matters of life and death, we aestheticize it—admiring order, pattern, interdependency, forces in tension or balance—and find a gratification in the complex, almost mathematical elegance of a system that is at bottom the simple, severe arithmetic of multiplication and subtraction. I am not suggesting that we grieve for the ants; nothing is "wronged" or treated unjustly by the way nature operates. It does not pose a moral issue that requires us to cultivate a different, somehow more appropriate response. But from a certain perspective, one we typically choose not to entertain, it is mildly terrifying. Without question, the mind and senses discover in nature a beauty, a refuge, even solace, but why should they find them in this fierce circle of mortality? Perhaps we merely insist on viewing the wild through our own preconceptions and desires, just as when we witness an act of predation we most often root for the prey. Or maybe we can afford to see these struggles as fascinating since they do not appear to involve us. Or possibly, in the way that so many human responses are strangely conjoined to their opposites, we recognize that a thing can be felt as both violent and beautiful at the same time, both tragic and ecstatic.

I have no answer, only an observation. Having spent more time considering the lilies than is generally regarded as seemly for a man of my age and circumstances, I understand that they are gloriously arrayed precisely because they, too, toil and spin. To be a lily is a great deal harder than it might appear, and I am damn glad not to be one of them.

"IN THE SOUL OF MAN"

there lies one insular Tahiti, full of peace and joy, but encompassed by all the horrors of the half known life.

—Herman Melville, *Moby-Dick*

I have a weakness for Melville; he speaks in the passionate certitudes and earnest finalities of youth, which are important to bear in mind even when they are wrong. But I understand what he means by a territory apart, a refuge that exists as both a real location and a space in the imagination, and that in both versions is surrounded by the rest of life, horrible, half known, or otherwise. At the calm center of the South Pacific, he found, at least for a time, a removal into the peace and joy he sought, and from the raw materials of the place he had discovered he fashioned the story that was lived there. Later, he wrote it down. Tahiti became his metonym for this place, the container that held his soul's desire.

In a more modest way, the Madison Valley has become mine. Bracketed by the work of the world on one side and the work of the wild on the other, in a separate territory between the two food chains, there exists a kind of middle space where I invent the place called Montana. It is not, as Melville would have it, entirely full of peace and joy—that is one of youth's necessary dreams—but it does possess these things in more than their customary proportions. These middle spaces of semidomestication took hold of my imagination in a time so long ago that I cannot even remember it, and I have looked for them whenever possible, and sometimes found them. Such places have accorded both a distance from the world of everyday living and a meaningful proximity to the natural one, and that trout streams have run through all of them has scarcely been a coincidence. Their borders have always enclosed as well a circle of close companions, those people in a life with whom spending time goes beyond a pleasure to become a species of necessity and for whom the middle space holds equal significance. Territories of this sort do not lie on some frontier, but they once did, and I have come to regard occupying them as a kind of homesteading, with the usual mixture of motives that have impelled such undertakings—partly a hopeful advance to the land of milk and honey, partly a tactical retreat to defensible high ground, half Tahiti and half Masada, located somewhere between the lilies of the field and the rest of your life, between grizzly bears and the Machine, an expanse of space and time that holds the remainder of the world on comfortably distant, though still distantly visible, perimeters.

What happens inside is by most measures, even our own, strikingly uneventful in the usual sense. We spend much of most days on the water, primarily on the Madison but sometimes elsewhere, often starting out around first light and not returning until midafternoon, or later if the fishing's good or we need to stop for supplies in town. Afterward, we convene beneath the cottonwoods out back and pursue the small employments of those whose imaginations and conversation, like the eyes of a raven, are drawn to shiny objects, to picking up and turning over whatever glittering bits of the world have come their way. The talk is interesting, which is only to say that it interests us, ranging widely until it turns up something worth lingering over awhile and then abruptly taking off again. Things can go on like this for quite some time, and these conversations always call to mind the rovings and pausings of an untrained bird dog at liberty to follow the whims of its nose, sometimes sniffing the scents of the larger world, sometimes muzzling through the duff of more personal matters, and sometimes, to all appearances, just rolling happily in the carcass of a dead salmon. But it always proceeds with the unaffected ease of longtime companions, and within such close familiarity, certain moments produce that indulgent sensation of being bathed in the conversation of friends. At other points, you feel more like a moving part in some unregulated contraption that speaks—one loosely put together, engineered to no discernible function, and successful primarily at a form of self-propelled chaos. This is enjoyable too. Sometime in early evening, the whole show moves indoors to the kitchen, where cooking and music get thrown into the mix and produce a minor bedlam of ten or twelve people bustling about at frenzied cross-purposes in a space designed for half the number. Dinner continues in this same approximate ambience, after which a general deceleration is experienced. Those less susceptible to the barbiturate aftermath of acute dining take a walk down the gravel road along the bench to watch the last of the sunlight climb the mountains and disappear into thin air.

All summaries by nature tend to the unremarkable, and perhaps this one especially. As I say, not a great deal happens. That's part of the whole point. And the time here is perhaps better described by how it is felt rather than spent, as ordinary days filled with the inordinate, one much like the next but each in its way brimming with irreproducible singularities.

The composition of our group changes almost constantly. Among the annual regulars, a handful of us remain for a number of weeks, while others show up at irregular intervals and overlap in random combinations.

Along with these, occasional visitors come out for a shorter stay or spend a few days on their way to somewhere else. The passing weeks bring a stream of arrivals and departures, trips to the airport in Bozeman, welcomings and farewells at the entrance to the gravel drive—but always in the aftermath, an animated company who differ profoundly from one another in many ways but are very much alike in a few important ones. And perhaps the most enduring consequence of this continual change, in the participants, in the experiences of the river and landscape each day, and even in the motion of solitary thought, is that the time spent inhabiting this middle space engages parts of one's self that ordinarily go underemployed in an equivalent interval of everyday life.

I find it, in short, among the most fully sufficient experiences of place that I have known, and at one time I wished it could continue indefinitely. But youth always seeks utopias and longs for them to last forever. Of that Tahiti in the soul, Melville warns: "God keep thee! Push not off from that isle, thou canst never return!" But of course he was young when he wrote that and got it backward. Pushing off is nonnegotiable; return is at best all you have. Metaphorical or actual, such places do not exist as permanences, at least for most people. Perhaps a few have found their island and never left. You can't really tell; they would hardly be in any great rush to advertise the fact. One imagines that they would be in no great rush to do anything. For the rest of us, the very impermanence of Tahiti makes it Tahiti in the first place, its value somehow tied up in transitoriness. At first, the temporariness of the circumstances carries with it an urgency to savor them as rare and wonderful, an awareness that itself casts things in a Tahitian light. But in time you arrive at the more somber and opposite truth and come to understand, as Robert Penn Warren writes: "The terror is, all promises are kept. / Even happiness." After that, you cannot help but feel poignancy in those places "full of peace and joy," or indeed in anything that you long for. They become both tragic and ecstatic.

There is nothing unique, or even exceptional, about any of this. To gather companionable society in an agreeable setting and let time off its leash for a bit appears to me a pretty fundamental human impulse. Most people would simply call it taking a vacation, and I wouldn't argue insofar as the core idea, "vacate," indicates an emptying out or leaving behind, since clearing a space to be filled by something else is to me intrinsic to the experience of place. But I have taken more vacations in the customary sense of the term than in retrospect may have been prudent, and the time spent here is rather different. "Recreation," understood literally as "making again," may finally be the better word for it, since the sense of restoration is a powerfully felt quality in this territory apart up on the benches. Exactly what gets restored can be difficult to explain; I doubt it's precisely the same for everyone, and in any case it occurs in recesses of the heart that can be articulated only in private terms. And most people, quite sensibly, don't really care to know you that well.

But this much I can say: that in this middle space, because of what and where it is, the days get lived with a greater deliberateness, which is to say with greater imagination. They have roots in an idea of locatedness that, as the essayist Franklin Burroughs describes it, "stretches back into the natural historical past, connecting it to the human and natural life of its present." A place may answer our longing to be claimed by locality, he observes, and be experienced as a kind of "inhabitable narrative," a story in which to participate. And in my own experience, such stories ultimately become reciprocal compositions, the mutual product of person and place, for as places evoke desire, so they are shaped by it, for better and worse.

As legions of academics would claw their way to a podium for the chance to explain, we in fact live inside narrative most of the time. The stories we tell order the past, explain the present, and give form to the future. We become characters in our own tales of ourselves—usually the hero, though in moments of candor possibly otherwise—and we fashion a narrative that gives meaning to a hero's exploits, whether triumphant or tragic, fixing them in that one particular story that will be remembered as how and why things happened. And to the extent of our capacities, more or less successfully, we arrange those elements within our control in order to tell, if not the best possible story, at least the one we want or need to hear.

But in the latitudes of the middle space the possibilities of narrative grow more plastic; the story can be shaped somewhat more in accordance with one's best imaginings for a richer experience of "the human and natural life of its present" and, one always hopes, for more and better fishing. Here, you find some play in the linkages of living that is unavailable in ordinary life, and it offers a greater liberty to invent the story as you go along in a way that makes it . . . well, more inhabitable. And more people take part in writing it. It does not involve some communal "experiment," or cultivated bohemianism, or pastoral idyll. The story has no plot in the conventional sense, nor is it a scripted or even conscious undertaking, but a kind of improvisation that becomes, in a way, the work of our play—to live a narrative of the potencies of place.

It is an ongoing story constructed from the raw materials of locality— from trout and rivers, from what you discover about them and from the unanswered questions they leave you with, from the particularities of a landscape on the edge of the wild, from small surprises that uncurl out of nooks of conversation and crannies of the day, from the meandering of ideas that roam about like animals let out of a zoo, and always from the apparently uneventful events of August afternoons spent beneath the cottonwood shade unhurriedly pursuing whatever tempts unsupervised curiosity—"doing nothing," as they say.

A two-day drive away, the Bodhi and the Intended are the last to arrive, their approach marked by a slowly advancing plume of gravel dust glimpsed a mile away through the Photographer's field glasses. It vanishes down a swale in the road, and at first we're not sure that it's them. Then the familiar scarlet stripe of a canoe materializes and levitates upward as the pickup truck to which it is lashed climbs a rise in the road. We walk from the shade into the heat of late afternoon and out beyond the wooden fence draped in waders to meet them at the drive. There is much commotion. From somewhere in the background comes the plosive burst of a champagne cork. Glasses appear. Everybody is talking at once.

2

OF CABBAGES AND KINGS

"The time has come," the Walrus said,
"To talk of many things:
Of shoes—and ships—and sealing-wax."
—Lewis Carroll, *Through the Looking Glass*
and What Alice Found There

IF ONE IS TO WRING EVERY LAST MOLECULE OF PLEASURE FROM AN EXPER-
ience—and I see no reason why that shouldn't be the case—one must
discover first what pleases best. Human desire's perverse capacity for self-
defeat can make such determinations difficult to arrive at, though I hasten
to add that some problems are worth having.

Very small trout streams and very large ones have this in common:
the best approach for introducing a fly to a fish presents few ambiguities.
You cannot boat down a tiny creek, and to advance upon the big water
in only waders and boots leads you mainly to deflating conclusions about
incongruities of scale. But the Madison, like many waters in southwest
Montana, is of a comfortable, democratic, middle size that accommodates
the wading angler and the drifting one equally. Moreover, both human
and natural agencies have rather neatly apportioned the stretch of river

between Quake and Ennis lakes. The uppermost and lowermost reaches, which offer better foot access and more productive wade fishing, have been declared off-limits to boat anglers, while the long middle segment, with its extensive stretches of private property, is more effectively and most often covered by floating. And so every evening back at the house, after dinner, we spend some time and no small effort on the question of who will do which on the following day. These deliberations, encumbered from the outset by postprandial narcosis and the dilemma of equally compelling alternatives, entail a complex calculus based upon the availability of oarsmen, rigs, and shuttle drivers; the recent fishing histories of various stretches of water; speculations about the coming day's weather; provisions that may need to be picked up on the way to or from fishing; shifting individual inclinations as the weeks progress; and always a scrupulous sense of equity that makes such negotiations deferential to the point of paralytic indecision, no one wanting to preempt the wishes of another. We frequently do not sort it out until the following morning at breakfast.

The Bodhi cartops a canoe, and the Photographer has a smallish raft and rowing frame, though we regard these as auxiliary craft to be used under specific circumstances. Floating the river is automatically understood to mean taking a drift boat. I've trailered a boat out every summer, though not always the same one. I acquired the first, a thirdhand sixteen-footer of obscure manufacture, in Oregon not far from the town where I live. Handsomely proportioned and light as a hopeful mood, it rode the water like a curl of duck down, and with two passengers in the front—the standard configuration in its region of origin—practically rowed itself. But with anglers fore and aft in the Rocky Mountain fashion, it handled like a coal barge, yet for reasons unknown skated around the river like a cottonwood seed in even the mildest breeze. Having seen long service and exhibiting what the antiques industry calls "condition issues," it required more upkeep than a British motorcycle. It is now someone else's fourth-hand boat, exchanged, along with a duffel bag full of currency in the higher denominations, for a lean, low-sided, modern, fifteen-foot assault craft deftly engineered to carry anglers at either end. Sleek and nimble, with spare and purposeful lines, it looks as businesslike as a rifle cartridge and rows like a racing scull, while offering luxury-class accommodations. It cannot match my first boat in innocence of heart, but for the requirements of Montana it has demonstrated its superiority in every other regard. Handling it is a joy, fishing from it happiness itself, and for all those kinds of reasons that go unmolested by logic, I would like to own several more. Boats are a lot like fly rods in this regard.

As rivers go, the Madison rows easily but not infallibly, its primary dangers posed by the varying skill levels of other oarsmen, which sometimes amount to approximately none. Having just launched one morning, the Bodhi and the Mechanic watched, stunned, as three fishermen backed down the boat ramp and dumped in a fifteen-foot aluminum V-hull rowboat, a craft only slightly better suited to the shallow, stony river than a tuna troller. The Mechanic pushed downriver, he and the Bodhi unwilling to play even the role of spectator in what would unquestionably come next. Not long afterward, anchored up to change flies, they watched a stream of life jackets, coolers, tackle boxes, and rubber flip-flops file past in silent mourning.

But barring this kind of thing, the river presents no great technical obstacles. As a rule, we take turns rowing during a day's drift, all except for the Cook, who has refused to learn how and each summer lays down the same casuistic smokescreen, arguing that getting proficient enough to squire his anglers with any competence at all would take weeks or more of practice, during which time he could not fish, and even we must concede the injustice of this. More importantly, he points out, coaching him through the drift would require the complete attentions of someone more experienced, and to deprive that person of fishing as well would be selfish and unthinkable.

In much the same spirit, the Cook will make an exaggerated show of helping to launch the boat, busying himself in an overstated fuss, and the instant the hull touches water hurdle into the front seat and the position of greatest fishing advantage. He justifies this with a familiar logic, arguing that he fishes badly from the stern, that he but dimly grasps the borders of his casting zone and would constantly cross lines with the angler in the bow, that much valuable time would be wasted in untangling his foul-ups or freeing his fly from the anchor rope, that this would send him into a funk, and that he has planned for tonight freshly baked white pizzas with handmade dough, lightly braised radicchio, portobello mushrooms, and a particularly nice Gorgonzola—a dish, we should be advised, he cooks poorly when depressed. The discussion usually ends there.

As far as catching fish goes, I find it hard to choose between wading and drifting. The difference lies less in the quality of sport than in one's perception of it, for they represent different orientations to the chase. On the most basic level, standing in the water makes you shorter; it lowers your line of sight, decreases the angle of vision, and the river presents itself in planar, horizontal terms. You come nearer to everything, especially the objects of greatest interest—the surface, whatever's floating on it, and the trout. Making headway in the current, fishing the water, and hooking and landing fish all involve a kind of close-quarters, physical participation, both a toe-to-toe meeting and an eye-level experience that feels immediate and visceral. This can play out in various directions. Under benign circumstances, it produces a pleasingly amphibious sense of puttering about in the water. But when the current is swift or deep, the traction dicey or the terrain rough, the wind or weather bad, fishing on foot can be more like an all-day bare-knuckle contest, though still a fair and proper stand-up match conducted according to the Marquess of Queensbury rules. Wade fishing rests on the deep psychology of righteousness and all the props available to the Man of Virtue in a classic morality play—self-denial, sacrifice, steadiness of character, endurance of hardship, humility, and the abnegation of worldly comforts. To wade the water is to participate in the ritual purification of bathing, one of the oldest and most widespread of metaphors, though ideally without the getting-wet part. In working a river on your own two feet you acknowledge that fishing actually involves getting your hands dirty; it is the most elemental and egalitarian way of addressing a trout stream.

Fishing from a drift boat has, by comparison, the aspects of high bourgeois. For one thing, there is a chauffeur. You have hot coffee in chilly weather and cold beer in the summer heat, a bulging hamper, cushioned seats, a comfortable place to put up your feet, and a convenient spot to set down your hors d'oeuvre or cigar should you rise to cast. And then, the vantage point is Olympian; the river unrolls beneath you like an aerial photograph, enhanced in depth and relief but with a similar sense of vertical distance and all the bankable advantages of elevation. Presenting a fly tends to the sanitary operations of the rooftop sniper or freelance asset trained to the head shot. Few targets lie beyond the range of a decent caster, and one can rather easily bend to this work with an almost soulless efficiency, at which point it's advisable to surrender the rod, grab the sticks for a while, and row until your head clears.

At the same time, drift-boat fishing demands a certain concentration, which is also part of the appeal. As each likely spot draws within reach—the soft water behind a boulder or the dark vertex of a bend—you must size up the configuration of the currents, compensate for the movement of the boat, compute the proper presentation in an instant, execute it in another, and then live with the results. A blown cast or bungled drift lies out there, dismally visible in the plain sight of God, a sad little turd in a teacup. A second chance does not always come, and a third almost never. If the current moves with any speed, as it does on much of the Madison, your spot and probably several other nice ones will have already slipped upriver, out of range and into the past. Each individual cast counts in a way that it does not for the wading angler. In some types of water, you might slow the boat or stop it momentarily, but even then you don't have quite the same sense of thoroughness that you do when wading, taking maybe five or six shots into a bucket that the man on foot might pound for an hour. So much good water passing so quickly can induce in the meticulous angler a moral discouragement, from feelings of waste and loss. You get in return, however, an uninterrupted supply of fresh river, endlessly novel permutations of current and obstruction in a succession of untried spots that seems functionally infinite. You fish on foot in high consciousness of the present, of the water in front of you at that moment; angling from a boat is very much about the future, about being always on the brink of getting one. Even in a boat, of course, a garden-variety shellacking is never far off, but new water has a way of sustaining expectations when the fishing is good and rebooting enthusiasm when it is not, and all this comes your way with remarkably little effort. Just lift the oars, and the boat will take you there, free of charge.

The prospect of new water certainly plays its part for the wading angler as well. But when the trout are up and taking, one has little inclination to move, and on a slow day, a change in venue is not apt to better the odds dramatically. Fishing on foot, at least as practiced by sane and sensible people, limits the territory available, and even though you may change locations, you're less likely to be fishing truly new water than just a new part of the old water. The results will probably look about the same. All fishing, of course, emanates from a fundamental hopefulness; the pessimist angles poorly and does not enjoy it. But not all hope takes the same shape. The sense of promise in wade fishing originates in its deliberateness, in the potential for adapting to circumstances, and in the confidence that every local angling problem has a solution. Answers do exist, though you must search for them. It is a complex form of hope, in its way shared by both science and theology, though disputes do arise about what actually constitutes an answer and how knowable it really is. The drifting angler, by comparison, embraces the more innocent optimism of what lies ahead, the fresh hand dealt, the next card turned; it is poker hope, by no means inferior but rather more easily purchased. For this reason, boating is quite popular.

My views on wading, of course, unavoidably reflect the way I happen to do it—which, to be brief, is less assertively than I used to. A decades-old knee injury that has returned like a bad check and a little limp in the equilibrium that I would like to attribute to an inner-ear malfunction instead of age have produced slight hesitancies and second thoughts in what used to come instinctively. None of this stops me; most of the time, it doesn't even make me more careful. But I have changed my game a bit, in the consciousness that a slipup which once would have involved a few quarts of cold inside my waders could now mean a one-way tumble down the currents of doom, particularly because I never learned to swim, at least as that term is commonly understood. I risk fewer of the chest-high, fast-water antics of the past, persuading myself that I now fish with greater cunning and stealth instead. Various little voices inside me know that this is a lie, and we never speak of it openly among ourselves.

But the fact remains that I work the water at a modest pace now, certainly faster than the more scrupulous and systematic Bodhi, though decidedly slower than the Mechanic, who fishes as though on wheels. All of us fish at a virtual standstill compared to a fellow we used to see on the river regularly over the course of several summers. Ropy and gangling, with a kind of extemporized anatomy that looked to have been assembled with a staple gun, he was perhaps in his forties during that time, skin as tan as saddle leather and sun-bleached streaks in long, frizzy hair that had apparently been attended to by a specialist in small explosions. Invariably clad only in nylon running shorts, wading boots, sunglasses, and sometimes a cotton bandanna knotted around his neck, he was a stitch or two away from legally nude, with a look more Malibu board jockey than fisherman and capable of inducing involuntary Beach Boys flashbacks. From all I could tell, he fished every day, and his routine never varied. After high-stepping out to the middle of the river, he would turn downstream and begin to wade, first in the semiweightless, quasicontrolled stumble of a man hustled along by a brisk current, then slowing his descent until the thigh-deep water piled to his waist on the upstream side.

He was a big-trout specialist, and his whole approach suggested a big-fish knowledge that had been distilled to a few uncomplicated principles. First, large trout eat large flies. Second, big fish live in big-fish water, which automatically discounts ninety-five percent of a river. And third, the first cast to a spot is the most critical and often tells the entire story; a large trout will take at once, or not, and no amount of subsequent persuasion will change its mind. This, of course, is only one theory, but on a river like the Madison, it succeeds often enough to account for his angling style: cover water; put one or two or, at most, three casts to only the best places; and— above all—keep moving. So he would chug steadily downriver, zigzagging as needed to intercept the prime water, hitting the trenches at the island heads, the deep runs along the banks, the dishes behind midstream shoals, the pockets and eddies. He would drop a big streamer into the heart of the matter and haul it back in long, sharp pulls, reefing on his fly line like a man starting a lawn mower. Except when he had a fish on, he never paused or stopped, but just kept on trucking downriver. I came to think of him as the Doo-dah Man and would sometimes see him, far from the nearest access point in either direction, disappearing around a bend, with miles to go before he slept. I doubt that, even back then, he was unique, and in the years since, his peripatetic style has become something of a fashion among younger anglers. But the Doo-dah Man was the first I saw to fish in a manner that, in keeping with the general minimalism of his whole approach, was a lot like floating the river but without a boat.

I most often encountered him during a day's drift, which can produce spectacles of several sorts, beginning at the boat ramp. At prime time in the morning, during the height of the summer season, a sizable fleet of drift boats, rafts, prams, and pontoon boats converge on the various launch points distributed up and down the river; boats are readied and line up for their turn at the water. And whenever people must wait, an escalating impatience can make them act in stupid and childish ways. Umbrages and resentments develop and express themselves in a subtle, retaliatory language of rig positioning, engine noise, and backup lights directed against those who dawdle at the ramp, or believe they have the seniority or importance or superior urgency to cut in ahead of the rest, or simply have no earthly conception of how the system works. Among the regulars who float the river every day, tiny private feuds may smolder on the periphery. These altercations rarely escalate into anything overt, but on a busy morning, the ramp will stage its little comedy if you know how to read the signs.

The crowd consists of guides, their clients, and recreational anglers like ourselves, whom I once overheard a guide refer to as "Joes," in tones that made clear we posed little impediment to the success of his own paying customers and mainly represented obstacles on the water around which one had to maneuver, much like big boulders but without trout behind

them. The guides stand out easily: uniformly game-faced, seldom openly
pleasant except to their clients, and just as seldom nakedly hostile, though
they run the gamut in other respects. The younger ones sport faux-tribal
ink around an ankle or bicep and the billowy, drooping pantaloons of
the Starbucks generation. The veterans, pearl-buttoned and permanent-
pressed under a trusty straw bucket, appear to have strolled from the set of
a singing-cowboy movie. Others look surprisingly like regular people. All
of them minister to the needs of their charges *du jour*, whose enthusiasm
and expectancy provide whatever exists in the way of a cheerful atmosphere
at the ramp. These days, more and more of the clients are women, whose
participation in fly fishing is, happily, on the rise. As a general philosophical
principle, I stand in favor of anything with more women in it, and their
presence alone enforces a certain minimum civility in the proceedings of
the morning.

A fair number of the guided anglers you see each summer were, only
moments before, nonanglers, which can be a handicap when fishing.
Among guides, the default routine involves knotting a beadhead nymph
a foot or two below a yarn strike indicator and imploring the beginner
to cast it as far as possible, which usually means within a rod length or
less of the boat. This is not exactly angling's deadliest technique, and
while I certainly do not feel sorry for these people—there's nothing here
to pity—I always feel a little discouraged on their behalf. But then an
inexperienced fly fisher, or a guide for that matter, can do little more under
the circumstances. And if the method does sometimes produce fish, it is
far more heartening to see that the fishermen almost always appear to be
enjoying themselves, which, if memory serves, is more or less the point of
it all and one of the few aspects of fly fishing in which beginners do not
find themselves at a disadvantage. When your paths cross on the river, they
prove refreshingly unschooled in the studied effronteries of the expert: the

unconcealed annoyance; the stink-eye stare and mumbled derogations; the defiant, territorial cast laid down in your fishing water like the peevish urinations of a house cat. Novices, on the other hand, tend to behave with the manners of well-intentioned people, waving and asking if you've had any luck, and should you return the question, they usually say the same thing: "Not yet!" You've got to admire that attitude—it's hard to catch fish without it—and I always enjoy seeing these newcomers on the river, though like most people, I'd much prefer to see no one at all.

You happen upon others, however, like the inexplicably somber, who stand in the boat at their stations front and rear in full expeditionary uniform—waders, vest, long-sleeved shirts buttoned at the cuff and collar, fingerless sun gloves, those Foreign Legion hats with the curtains in the back, expressionless faces lathered in blinding quantities of white zinc oxide cream—and they drift toward you, fly rods waving, like some surreal floating Kabuki. The guide, his tight-lipped visage weathered to the aspect of a crocodile change purse, has the concrete gaze and robotic gestures of a man who's pumped the same lever on the same widget press for a few too many weeks in a row. Well or poorly, they fish in silent earnestness, as though something of dreadful importance depends on it, and a palpable intensity radiates from the boat like a force field. It is always a relief to see this tension punctured, as not uncommonly happens, by a flotilla of little kids from town who come bobbing into sight on fluorescent inflatable horsies, giggling past the boat in high counterpoint to the scene, and bouncing down the current around a bend like a clutch of ducklings. You see this sort of thing wading, too, but it seems to pass by you more quickly.

People being what they are, conflicts inevitably crop up between those in boats and those not. Usually avoidable but not always avoided, they generally take the predictably American form of one indignant sense of entitlement confronting another, and sometimes you wonder whom to pull for. The obstinate wade fisherman, planted in the middle of the only navigable slot in the river and resolved to defend his claim, probably deserves the fate of all those people who believe that being right is somehow preferable to remaining in one piece. At the same time, the angler on foot is almost universally the injured party. One can forgive the offenses of an unskilled oarsman if the apologies due are fully and sincerely paid. But the one who deliberately drifts through the wading angler's water or instructs his passengers to poach it from a distance should be garroted with his own anchor rope and the boat scuttled. Surprisingly, clients will sometimes defuse such situations and look at you apologetically, in obvious mortification at the rudeness of their guide, which they recognize even though they've never fished before in their lives. Between you passes a wordless acknowledgment that some people are simply assholes and there's no future in getting worked up about it. Busy days on the river, though, can suck you into this kind of thing involuntarily, and I confess to having launched a brush-back pitch or two with a tungsten conehead at some boat that was determined to fish all the best water, including mine, or wouldn't veer around it out of sheer laziness. But such skirmishes seldom amount to much. Harsh words may get exchanged from time to time, but one rarely sees anything involving fists, and nothing really to speak of in the way of gunplay. Altercations generally last for only the brief moments it takes a drifting boat to pass a stationary fisherman, though hard feelings do linger on. As with rush-hour driving or the public use of cell phones, everyone believes we need a code of etiquette, but no one can agree on what it would be, and some couldn't bring themselves to observe it regardless.

Most encounters on the river, however, do not involve people and so hold a greater interest. It astonishes me, for instance, how closely you can approach animals when you are floating. Deer in particular treat you more as a minor curiosity than anything else, a mildly bewildering novelty rather than a threat. Perhaps with the instincts of terrestrial creatures, they fail to register danger coming from the water, or maybe, half-concealed by brush on the bank, they think themselves invisible. You can watch them watching you drift nearer, heads swiveling to follow you as you pass, lower jaws grinding away at a mouthful in that odd, elliptical style of mastication. If you remain quiet and hold the oars still, you can draw within yards of them before they disappear into the trees. Perhaps they've merely grown accustomed to the constant boat traffic, but I have observed pretty much the same thing on almost every river I've floated. Their insouciance appears to be biological rather than learned. Waterfowl, by contrast, are somewhat cagier, suspicious and edgy. Herons fidget as you get nearer until they can no longer bear it, then take to the air in slow, prehistoric gestures and somehow, with their second-story center of gravity and the wrong kind of feet, alight delicately in the trees and croak their throat-clearing call. The big raptors—bald and golden eagles, osprey, red-tailed hawks—perched in snags or on jackleg fences, behave with the same indifference as the deer. Mink can be wary, but muskrats aren't much bothered, and the gregariousness of otters is legendary. They seem to intuit instantly that a boat is slow, ungainly, and pitifully unmaneuverable compared to their lithe and handsome selves and so presents little cause for alarm.

Half-expected but always a surprise, such things come and go along the river. And even though you spend a float trip in almost constant motion, it feels more episodic than serial, a collection of particular moments rather than a continuous narrative, perhaps because you see more than you can take in, or perhaps because some segments of every fishing day are, to be honest, unmemorably spent and you take little notice of them. Whatever the reason, the experience of drifting has, overall, a cinematic character, a montage of constantly shifting scenes as the river and day spool out ahead of you. And the Madison Valley offers a wide-screen presentation, a landscape of open range or sloping hills receding to a panorama of mountains in the distance. As a way of seeing the river, drifting is altogether charming in the original meaning of "casting a spell over," with a lulling sense of being borne effortlessly along.

Taking the path of least resistance in a boat means remaining in motion; on foot, however, it means moving as little as possible. Gaining or maintaining ground in the current always involves some degree of hindrance from the water, and practically speaking, the river becomes a smaller place. You pay more attention to less of it, and as a result, fishing on foot invites an investigatory pace that makes legible a world close-up and profusely detailed. Few places I know of better reward the angler in this respect than those miles of the Madison I have already mentioned where the many islands—some large and wooded, others small and thick with brush—subdivide the water into a broad fan of capillaries, each a small stream distinctly its own and often too narrow or shallow or troublesome to negotiate in a boat. Though hardly unvisited, these side channels are among the less disturbed places on the river, and because of them, each stream mile may cumulatively contain six or eight miles of riverbank, that middle space of edge habitat where wonders occur.

Not many summers ago, I found myself at the margin of a low, triangular patch of grass on the tail of a comma-shaped island, fishing a cutbank run. Though not large, the water had it all—the depth, the flow, the look—and I spent quite some time standing in one spot casting, and changing flies, and not catching fish in half a dozen different ways, until an abrupt commotion distracted me. Only a few feet away, an adult killdeer began thrashing about at the water's edge, dragging first one wing and then the other, leaping wildly up and down, shrieking in distress, and generally performing the injured-wing act with such conviction that I feared it might actually injure itself. I finally noticed in the grass at my feet an indistinct, careening little flurry of mottled-brown fuzz that eventually sorted itself out into four or five tiny killdeer chicks. They couldn't have been much more than a few days old, each small as a cotton ball, with a tiny black chevron of beak and glossy India-ink eyes and no more substance than a dollop of whipped egg white. Something about my wading boots incited the keenest interest, and they swarmed over my shoe tops, pecking at invisible things on the laces, all the while emitting almost ultrasonic peeps that spurred their mother to ever more frantic demonstrations. Reluctant to move my feet, pinned to the spot by the weight of their uncomprehending fragility, I finally lowered my fly rod, reel first, and, with the gentlest of possible swings, putted them off my boots one by one, at which point they tottered off elsewhere. You don't necessarily expect this kind of thing when wading a trout stream, but on those fortunate days, just this kind of thing comes your way.

Regardless of how I encounter a river, from the deck of a boat or on the soles of my feet, I've always felt this about being there: you don't just see more, you see better. Perhaps because of the way water bends and bounces and transmits light—as prism and pane, mirror and lens—fishing possesses not only a visual dimension but an optical one. Floating a river has a telescopic quality, as far-off things—the pool ahead, the next bend, the island in the distance—are continually brought nearer to you. Fishing on foot has a microscopic character and makes small things into large ones. Boots and boats represent as much instruments of observation as methods of getting around. Fly fishing is not one of the eternal verities, but it can bring you closer to a few, the stream itself foremost among them. There is a certain and distinct pleasure, the source of which I cannot pinpoint, in simply watching water run downhill, an endless scroll of current on which the river inscribes the complicated history of itself. And it reads equally well whether you choose to be in the water or on it. It merely comes down to a matter of what pleases best, and once that is resolved, no other relevant questions remain.

But there is one last thing. When I was growing up, my family traveled to a lake in the far north of Wisconsin for a week or two each summer. The four kids would spend endless hours either up to our necks in the water, swimming and horsing around, or bobbing about in a rowboat catching panfish. But no matter how I passed the day, what I remember most vividly is lying in bed at night with the sensation of being surrounded by water, skin rippling with the feel of imaginary waves, the nodding swell over and underneath me, the soft pulsing of the lake still remembered by nerve and muscle. And even now, after a day of feeling the pressure of current against me or the rocking of water through the hull of a boat, I have much the same sensation of dropping off to sleep with the river still around me. In an odd way, this may be one of the reasons I fish.

3

BACK AT THE RANCH

The frailty of our human bodies and the advantage of our opposable thumbs make buildings so necessary and possible that they don't seem artificial at all. Instead, they seem an extension of the earth's circumstance and our own being in the world.

—Ann Cline, *A Hut of One's Own*

THE HOUSE WE OCCUPY UP ON THE BENCHLAND NO LONGER MAKES UP part of a ranch, though it once did, and in houses as in people, the past persists. A few machine sheds and outbuildings, livestock pens, and a wooden cattle chute all speak of a former life, of a place someone else invented. In a field out back, the weathered carcass of an old seed drill rusts in the sun, the fingers of spiraled steel and the iron pelvis of its saddle now half grown over in wild mustard and yellow clover. A table top of grazing land extends from the house in all directions, most of it part of a few working ranches off in the distance. Thick biscuits of rolled hay stacked beyond a rail fence to the south smell of must and sun. Angus cattle sometimes wander up to the three-strand barbed wire on the north edge, the young ones bellowing inconsolably amid the cloud of flies that follow them everywhere. More often, a few deer or a solitary antelope nibble around the wooden posts and, without warning or a running start, vault the fence like they were launched from an underground silo, expending no more apparent effort than a man stepping over a crack in the sidewalk.

Although flanked by the high drama of mountains on the east and west and open to a long view of the valley between them, the few square miles of territory that encircle us present the kind of undifferentiated countryside that practically defines open grasslands, and the fence lines that divide it seem comically arbitrary in their efforts to separate a great deal of one thing from a lot more of the same. By no means a featureless landscape, its features lean to the subtle and spare—a swale or swell, a rock outcrop, the tree line of the river in the distance. And like all landscapes, this one contains its beauties, which is a lucky thing because there is much of it.

But for entirely artificial reasons, the small plot of land on which the house sits looks very unlike the rest. A narrow channel, perhaps a yard wide at most and dug to carry irrigation water to the fields beyond, borders the house on three sides. The water doesn't flow continuously; it may run one week and not the next, according to where and when it's needed. But by the middle of the summer, the small headgate at the corner of the property generally stays at least partially open. The first year we arrived at the ranch, we found growing along the bank a single fork-toothed ookow, a lanky, foot-tall flower with a ball-like burst of violet-blue blooms, and the Painter began referring to this trickle of water as Blue Dick Creek, after the common name of the plant. I've no idea how a flower might come to be called this, but just as a precaution, I have never touched it. One portion of this channel wanders along behind the house in shallow serpentine arcs rather than the point-to-point linearity one might expect in something so utilitarian. I've never been able to determine if it was dug in this fashion out of some sense of the picturesque—there would seem no other reason to do it—or whether, in the way of all moving water, it began to meander on its own. Whatever the reason, its gentle curvatures, low gradient, and overhanging grasses do a fairly convincing impression of a miniature spring creek. Nowhere more than ankle-deep, the current trickles quietly but audibly over a bed of rounded stones, and the sound of moving water never fails to improve the acoustics of a place.

In this arid country with barely a foot of annual precipitation, any reasonably reliable source of moisture is quickly exploited by the needier forms of vegetation that cannot gain a foothold in drier soils. And the most notable consequence of this little ribbon of water are the volunteer cottonwoods and a few planted pines that have taken root along the banks, grown tall, and now ring the house and its plot of land in a horseshoe of trees. This kind of wooded setting, while not altogether unique, appears only rarely amid the broad, open land of the benches, and on an August afternoon the trees cast a blessed shade, the leaves sift a hot wind into a thousand smaller breezes, and the air around Blue Dick always feels cooler, though I may just be imagining this last part. But whether you view them from a distance or sit underneath them looking out, the trees produce the overwhelming impression of an island of green amid a late-summer sea of sere and bleached grasses. It is an insular space, partly created and partly spontaneous, distinctly oasis-like, a kind of Tahiti.

As a rule, I divide the theoretical constructs of the social sciences into the impenetrable and the implausible, but on occasion they end up making a rough sort of sense. A few decades ago, the countercultural anarchist writer Peter Lamborn Wilson, working under the pseudonym Hakim Bey—a man regarded in some quarters as a bit of a crackpot and in others as borderline lunatic but whose notions are intriguingly offbeat—described a particular type of group relationship that exists outside of institutional mechanisms of social control. He coined a term for it: the "temporary autonomous zone." Bey enjoys more a cult status than an establishment credibility—just as an anarchist would prefer, I imagine—and his work is most often invoked these days in discussions of such cultural apogees as all-night raves, the Burning Man festival in Nevada's Black Rock Desert, and the various Naughty Santa escapades that inspired a minor underground vogue among the self-styled "santarchists." As originally put forth, the idea of the temporary autonomous zone came freighted with the political or, more accurately, anti-political associations of uprising and insurrection, which in certain contexts have their allure. But taken at face value, the term "temporary autonomous zone" has a usefully calibrated objectivity about it. I admit that this concept is a rather heavy piece of machinery to turn loose on a group of friends gathered for a few weeks in the Montana hinterlands. But I wheel it out because it has a quirky sort of appropriateness and because it runs without the fuel of nostalgia or the lubrications of sentimentality.

As unfamiliar and curiously formal as it may sound, the term gives a name to what I suspect falls within the experience of many people and maybe most. It describes a kind of communally created pocket of emancipation, an envelope of liberatedness that is partly physical, partly psychological, and perhaps even partly spiritual in a strictly nonsectarian sense, since autonomy has been found not to mix well with the orthodoxies of any major denominations. Such spaces exist apart from the ordinary world, sometimes literally, sometimes figuratively, but always by devaluing the usual structures on which that world relies—conventions, conformities, norms, proprieties, and protocols, as well as the more tangible forms of authority that keep the system humming. These zones take shape instead around a sense of being the sovereign of yourself, "the monarch of your own skin," as Bey puts it, and in this respect I suppose they technically qualify as a form of anarchy—possibly benign, possibly not, depending as always on the monarch. Our own version of the temporary autonomous zone probably amounts to little more than what he characterizes as simply a group of people harmonizing "their efforts to realize mutual desires, whether for good food and cheer, dance, conversation, the arts of life," or even, as he explains, "to create a communal artwork," of which the inhabitable narrative could be seen as modest form. And perhaps the most fundamental theme of that story is, to borrow a more respectable term from anthropology, the enjoyment of *communitas*, a heightened state of togetherness and mutuality, a participation in the informal rituals of a pleasing place and time, and that feeling of richly charged occasion that often informs a gathering of longtime friends.

We have no flaming human effigy to symbolize this. Building one always seemed like too much work. Rather, if we have fashioned anything like a space of autonomy in this landscape of range and river, the small stand of trees and the house among them are the emblem and agent of its making.

The house itself is of an unprepossessing sort, in appearance equally distant from the manufactured anonymity of the standard American tractburger and the synthetic rusticity of the modern western ranchette. It is an in-between kind of place, a slightly boxy, single-story frame structure you would probably take no note of when driving past except perhaps to remark on its fortunate situation among the trees. With its back to the river valley, it faces, though at some remove and through a screen of pines, the lightly traveled gravel road that runs by in earnest, linear purposefulness to nowhere in particular. Windows in the living room and kitchen look out in the same general direction, while the rear of the house, with its magnificent view, has no windows of public significance. The only concessions to the natural setting come in the form of a raised wooden porch in back, just large enough for a few chairs and, beyond it, a small plot of grass under the cottonwoods, both of which look out on an expansive panorama of the Madison Range. In both the unpretending architecture and the citylike orientation toward the road, it looks much like an ordinary residence in a town, what in plain language you would call a "regular house," as opposed to a "recreational property." And though I know little of the history of this place beyond our own occupation of it, I can imagine the original owners as ordinary people, working and raising a family, not insensitive to the great natural beauty around them but living here primarily for other reasons.

The interior of the house tells a similar story and, beyond a familiar everyday comfort, holds nothing especially remarkable except a large and handsome fieldstone fireplace built from local schists and gneisses of dusty blue-greens, rust-streaked ochres, and rich charcoals flecked in cream and pale rose. Its one other feature of note showed up just recently: an advanced-technology, water-saving toilet that flushes with the sound of an erupting volcano and never fails to provide newcomers with a memorable lavatory experience. Otherwise, the place has been neither designed nor appointed in decorator fashion nor aestheticized in the manner of real-estate-brochure "western vacation homes," with wagon wheels, horse traces, branding irons, or other appurtenances intended to evoke a sense of "period" or "heritage." The rooms contain instead the material objects of everyday living, and though none of these belong to us, we have over the years acquired a history of sorts with them; they've grown familiar, and should something new appear or something old vanish, it does not go unnoticed. The contents of a house inevitably speak of its owners, their likes and dislikes, tastes and aversions, needs and interests, possibly their politics, and sometimes their sense of humor, which in this case leans to the wry and ironic. The Segals live out of state, residing here only intermittently, and countless small details suggest that the time is spent happily and, I've always thought, in much the same spirit as our own.

Though the house is not ours, it serves for a while as our home space, and in a certain respect, occupying it resembles a high grade of camping—not in any primitiveness of accommodations, but in the creation of a temporary and improvised domesticity. In a borrowed place, you may stay for an extended time, but you cannot move in to any deep degree or problems arise when it comes to extricating yourself. Important things get left behind. By the same token, you have leisure enough to justify living beyond a suitcase, spreading out a bit, and, as the expression goes, making yourself at home. As quarters go, these are not large and we are sometimes numerous, and under these circumstances, space and the allocation of it become matters of the common weal. We each need somewhere to park a few weeks' worth of stuff, to sleep, and occasionally to retreat to—a place specified by actual walls if possible and if not by mutual accommodation or, when things get really crowded, an imaginary line drawn between the green chair and the corner of the TV set. By long-standing custom, the Painter and I have the largest of three bedrooms; the Cook and the Writer, who is also his wife, occupy the next in size. The Mechanic, along with any shorter-term residents such as the Hindu, take the smallest of the three, which has come to be known, somewhat unfairly I feel, as the Hole, since it's a trifle deficient in outside light and ventilation, though in the main altogether serviceable. This particular space has become something of a conversation piece, and though much sport is made of it, and by extension its occupants, I myself have spent a few nights in the Hole. It's not all that bad, though I much prefer the standing arrangements. Whatever other visitors, associates, or passers-through that arrive locate themselves wherever they can find room.

Although he is my brother, the Bodhi has the genes of a Bedouin and, even if the house has room available, prefers to sleep in a tent—specifically when he comes to Montana, but more generally under circumstances where normal people would seek out a motel room or the couch of a friend for the night. He shares this tent with the Intended since she has similar, if not quite as enthusiastic, inclinations. They pitch it at a corner of the property near the trees, in the mostly unsuccessful hope of sheltering it from the screaming winds that sometimes descend into the valley and have, over time, flexed the tent poles into graceful and permanent aluminum parentheses. The Photographer, too, comes equipped with his own shelter, one that represents the most current solution in his eternal quest for ideal mobile accommodations. He has run through a succession of small campers and travel trailers that function as bunkhouse, kitchen, portable photo studio, and fly-tying room, never keeping one longer than a few years before its limitations become unendurable or something better comes along. He has a strong streak of perfectionism and in this regard much resembles the Mechanic, who arrives each summer and immediately searches for something to fix or, if nothing needs repair, something to tune or tweak or refurbish or improve upon. In his world, everything could stand to be better than it is, and making it so has become something of a personal mission.

A large wooden table takes up most of the dining room and serves both as a makeshift library for the several crates of field guides and assorted books that make the trip every summer and as a fly-tying bench, which by any rational measure should be unnecessary. One of my functions, also by long-standing custom, is to provide flies for everyone, some of whom fish the better part of most days, and a few nearly all day every day. To that end, I bring along eight or ten large, multicompartment stock boxes full of dry flies; two of streamers; and at least half a dozen more of nymphs. By conservative estimate they contain somewhere around four thousand flies, though this figure is misleading. Specialty patterns account for a great many of them—flies we never use, tied for trout we never catch, rising to hatches we never see—while others, designed for more catholic purposes, have simply never produced much.

I lug these freeloaders along in part because I would feel underequipped without them, but mostly because it is axiomatic in fly fishing that the hottest pattern is always the one you don't have. So these flies operate through a kind of preemptive exclusion, narrowing the search for the patterns that will work by reliably indicating those that won't, and the more losers you have on hand, the more quickly you will converge on the right stuff. In their fashion, then, they achieve the essential aim of all trout flies, which is to catch trout—it just won't be on these. This logic explains perhaps eighty percent of the flies I bring, and some of these veterans have been making the trip to Montana for as long as I have. The remainder consists of those unsurprising choices—grasshoppers, Stimulators, Royal Wulffs, Princes, Woolhead Sculpins, and so on—that, while hardly infallible, make reasonably dependable bets. In times of good fishing, we can exhaust the supply of these—hence the fly-tying gear.

I have another motive for it as well. It has been a minor objective of mine, and a form of petty vanity, that no one who comes out to fish should have to buy, or technically even own, any flies. The Mechanic seems determined to frustrate this ambition and arrives at the house each summer with a few dozen of the indispensable patterns *du jour* culled that very day from the several local fly shops he visits on the drive out. And while most of them look to me like credit-card candy for the tourists, I will nevertheless duplicate some of these at the vise and add the rest to the stock-box list for the following summer. Something of a competition has developed between us—I attempting to preclude any future purchases on his part, and he, as far as I can tell, just trying to wear me down. I have no hope of winning, of course, but looking forward to a fishing trip and preparing for it bestows a happiness of its own, and the flies I tie represent the material form of my private anticipatory pleasure.

They constitute, however, only a tiny portion of the mythic heaps of tackle that travel with us. We bring several rods and reels apiece, waders and boots and rain gear for all, vests and day packs, a large cardboard carton or two of fishing-related accessories and second-tier tackle items, and, naturally, multiple spares, backups, and extras of everything from boat anchors to boot laces. That the town of Ennis may well contain more fly shops per capita than anywhere else in the world and with them the instant satisfaction of any conceivable fly-fishing-related need or whim never enters into our thinking. A necessary component of autonomous spaces, and one of their central enjoyments, is a sense of independently functioning self-containment. We extend this principle to the matter of provisions as well and arrive every summer fortified with boxes of food, beverages by the case, crocks of olives, sacks of coffee and spices, blocks of cheese, and various other requirements of good living, a fair amount of which could be readily procured in town. We warehouse this substantial inventory of equipment and supplies in what could properly be called a utility room, since it not only contains a washing machine and dryer, but, in fact, furnishes a space of great utility. Part granary and part armory, it is conveniently accessed through the back door, sufficiently high-ceilinged to admit a fully assembled fly rod, and large enough to store coolers; so the room has become the default staging area for daily trips to the river and in the mornings is quite a busy place. All in all, it looks something like a cross between a sporting goods store and an air-raid shelter and provides effective containment for a reservoir of stuff that, if left undammed, would swamp the house in a knee-deep slurry.

We also make use of the basement, which functions for us much like the downstairs of the church, where the pews used to be, in "Alice's Restaurant." It provides a temporary cache for empty boxes and bottles and the other assorted butt ends of our days and ways that will, in a day or two, certainly by the end of the week—say, the beginning of next week at the absolute latest—be hauled away to the town dump.

Anthropologists will tell you what you already know intuitively: that a house defines the most elemental of all human spaces. We have grown quite fond of this one, in its quirks and foibles and in its pliant generosities. Our presence here is in part, inevitably and crucially, a domestic one, and the most inhabitable domestic spaces yield to the changing needs of whomever inhabits them and yet somehow remain fundamentally themselves. They possess an organic quality, participating in the expansions and contractions of human experience and often recording the important ones. A house will tell its own story and, in doing so, become part of your own. The best ones achieve their eloquence not through some studied elements of design but precisely because their spaces are undesigned, ordinary ones—"authentic places," Ann Cline calls them.

Some time ago, the Painter and I lived for a couple of years in a tiny house we heated mainly with wood burned in an odd and deceptively sized Swedish-made stove, small but capable of glowing ferocities. Despite some early misgivings, I discovered that I liked it immensely, splitting and hauling the wood, starting a fire each morning and tending it through the day. Even the idea of it had a pleasing, if largely illusory, off-the-grid feeling. But I hadn't at all expected that what I would most value about the stove was its localized point of warmth and radially declining slope of temperature, an almost solar geometry, so unlike furnace heat, which is nondirectional, everywhere at once, and devoid of interesting shape. It made me aware of other such point sources in a house and how, without realizing it, I automatically favored them—how the bright spot of a floor lamp in a dark room, its intensity dissipating with distance, appealed more than the homogeneity of overhead light; how the breeze from a window open next to me suited better than the uniformity of air conditioning. Gradients create variation and texture in a space—heat and cool, light and shadow, stillness and motion. I enjoy the feel of them, their sense of distinct origin and increment, and have come to appreciate the character of domestic spaces partly in these terms.

In the house at the ranch, as in a great many houses, the point source of communal emanation—its flame, filament, and breeze—is the kitchen, the archetypal domestic space. Much takes place here. It is the first meeting place of the morning and often the last at night. Fishing plans are made and revised and finalized here. After coming back from the river, we collect around the kitchen table for a time before retreating to the shade of the trees. The first anglers to return pull up chairs, fix a bite to eat and something to drink, talk over the day's fishing and speculate about tomorrow's until a second bunch arrives, sits down, and gives an account of its own, and so on until all the stragglers have straggled in. This accumulation can take a leisurely while, so we end up logging a lot of time around the kitchen table, losing track of the clock. As the group grows larger, the table becomes insufficient, and some end up leaning against countertops or in doorways. But we never think about moving elsewhere in the house, away from this hospitable space with its large windows, airiness, and sunlight. Nearly always, music is playing—sometimes the object of deliberate listening, sometimes receding into the background and advancing again as the conversation swells and subsides. The Bodhi and the Intended assume primary responsibility for engineering what is called in the more academic circles of the art world—and you really have to hand it to these people—the "sonic architecture" of our experience. The two of them have the biggest music collection, though almost everyone chips in something for the general consideration of the rest. Every other day or so, the Writer bakes fresh bread, and the kitchen becomes especially popular.

On most nights, later in the evening after the conclusion of the video portion of our entertainment, which consists mostly of documentaries about music or musicians, the kitchen comes alive again, albeit on a smaller scale. One or two of us—most often the Cook and the Mechanic—will snap on the light and sit down at the kitchen table, which automatically attracts two or three others. Añejo and ice cream make frequent appearances. The talk starts up and roams around, often assuming a more intimate character and running well into the night. At these hours, the kitchen is a kind of unregulated zone, an open territory even for the mice, who grow fearless and skitter about euphorically on the linoleum. Voices and laughter, held low in deference to those already asleep, radiate outward from the kitchen in a steady decrescendo, from the sense of words to the sound of syllables to a low murmur that washes over the floors into the far corners of the house.

But a kitchen finds its highest and best expression in the purpose for which it was designed, the preparing of food, which in the mornings is apt to be informal, though not without its ritual observances. Most days, the Mechanic busies himself with blueberry pancakes, each fresh berry hand-placed in a painstaking, one-per-forkful precision to which he attaches almost mystical importance. Each individually made pancake strains the capacities of a twelve-inch skillet, dwarfs a dinner plate, and weighs slightly less than a regulation discus. He and the Cook, practiced trenchermen both, will dispatch a couple of these apiece, topped with an ingot of butter and proportionate quantities of the kind of syrup that comes from actual trees. The rest of us breakfast on a human scale, while the Writer grinds coffee beans from a closely guarded personal stash and prepares espresso in a special pot she keeps close about her at all times, as one might insulin or an inhaler. The Cook, a reluctant but resigned enabler of this Balzacian jones, heats the milk and reminds her that the caffeine junkie is an appalling cliché for someone in her line of work.

Cooking dinner is a joint enterprise and a focal event on most days. As late afternoon turns to early evening, the kitchen ramps up to a scene of barely controlled chaos in which everyone participates, usually under the direction of the Cook, who interprets his administrative responsibilities broadly, not only coordinating the work of hands but fostering and furthering the great good humor that prevails. So far in my life, I've been acquainted with three naturally gifted cooks, their native aptitudes cultivated through practice rather than formal training, and each of the three slightly different. One works from an acute understanding of ingredients—vegetables, fishes, meats, and seasonings—knows their natures and behaviors, and grasps the deep logic of the various techniques for preparing them. The second has exceptionally discriminating senses of taste and smell that allow him to dissect even complex dishes into their native components and proportions, and to reproduce memorable meals from his memory of them. But the one I've known the longest is the Cook, who brings to the table an inventive type of spontaneity and counts among his more enviable talents the ability to consult an uninspired or even functionally bare-naked larder and still conjure up something to feed the multitudes in style. I believe he sees it as a form of puzzle and takes pleasure in solving it.

More typically, though, we have a dinner concept, with the materials to execute it stocked in advance. Table and countertops are cleared to make space, and everyone sets to work. Being considerably more particular about kitchen steel than our culinary skills warrant, we bring our own knives, along with cutting boards, garlic presses, graters, juicers, double-barreled baguette pans, and the various specialized, redundant, and often superfluous gadgets that can make amateur cooking a lot like fly fishing. None of us inclines to the more precious forms of haute gastronomy in which six or eight hand-selected flavor molecules lie artfully composed on a baby leaf of green tea flown in still dewy from Jiangsu, garnished with a hieroglyph of a krill-embryo reduction, then served with a *chawan* of jasmine-scented steam and a tiny silver straw through which the whole meal may be enjoyed in a single snort. Our eating wanders erratically through various ethnic and domestic cuisines, but the flavors are always big and vivid and, to the farthest extent possible under the circumstances, fresh. Strangely, and I mention this as a point of peculiarity rather than moral vanity, we have never once eaten trout, despite our unanimous conviction that twenty years of never keeping a single fish has entitled us to one modest dinner of brown trout, sautéed or grilled. But when the moment of truth arrives on the river, we can't quite bring ourselves to summon the priest or, in the inadvertently perceptive words of the state fishing regulations, catch a fish and "reduce it to possession." No one should kill a trout without a sense of having diminished the world's quotient of wildness. This isn't necessarily a reason to renounce the practice, but if it doesn't give pause, you have some things to think about.

Once or twice a summer, the Hindu, who stays only a week or so, masterminds a meal—always labor-intensive East Indian food, for which the better part of a day must be set aside. One aspect of these preparations that I have come to appreciate is the suspense that surrounds them, as the Hindu, who has a penchant for the theatrical, conceals until the last possible moment the number and nature of the dishes under construction.

If pressed, he will reveal all but prefers that you don't ask. And so we proceed on our uninformed way: one of us chops a half bushel of onions, while someone else peels oranges, another washes spinach, another seeds chilies or slices lemons, someone does something or other to chickens; garlic roasts in the oven, lentils soak, heaps of basil and cilantro and golden raisins wait on the counter next to a bowl of chickpeas and one of heavy cream. Dough is rolled out, and the Hindu himself toasts, grinds, and mixes spices—cumin, black and yellow mustard seed, turmeric, coriander, garam masala, cayenne, fenugreek, and the smallest pinch of asafetida with its smell of pulverized gym socks. All the pieces lie in plain sight, but the big picture remains a mystery.

We may begin all this immediately after lunch to leave time for the simmering and braising and roasting that will follow. The Hindu is a student of the stomach and also no fool, and at some point around midafternoon the Mechanic lights a grill on the back porch, bowls and platters are carried out, and it becomes clear that a small detachment of galley slaves has been unknowingly occupied in forestalling a starvation-induced riot. Space is cleared on the table, and suddenly food arrives—papadams and chutneys, maybe, or fire-roasted eggplant with garlic and olive oil. We crowd around and eat. A corkscrew appears and the music is nudged up in volume to rise over the clink of glasses. The Hindu entertains us by re-creating classic moments in Bollywood film or telling impenetrable jokes from the motherland: "Okay, a Smartha and a Shakta walk into a bar . . . " Thus fortified, we return to the matters at hand until they are finished.

In the end, I find it curious that while the English lexicon currently contains about one million words, some fraction of which catalog our desires and loves, licit and otherwise, not a single one of them to my knowledge names the very particular pleasure of being together and cooking. The word "conviviality" may come closest, but I still find it inadequate to this considerable task. Perhaps they do better in other languages. I wonder, though, whether we would feel the same urgency for either art or cooking if we had precisely the right word for expressing absolutely everything.

Food is, in one respect, a drug, and a really good meal is like a really good drug, a narcotic rush that gradually glides down to a comatose, slow-motion contentment. But it requires proper company; without that ingredient, one consumes even the best of meals with the mechanical joylessness of a man scarfing Stop 'N Shop doughnuts on his drive to the office. Dinners at the ranch are spirited and companionable affairs where, among other things, "the world is examined, plots hatch, cheeses are passed, life's joy and regrets slosh around with the cognac," as Ellen Meloy says. Like cooking, they are events of high conviviality and the essence of *communitas*. And there is a word for this, at least after a fashion: "gastrosophy." It came into use during the nineteenth century, not coincidentally about the same time that America was awash in a wave of the utopian schemes that have always been a part of our cultural landscape. A number of these visions of model living coalesced around the newfound "science" of gastrosophy, a kind of you-are-what-you-eat philosophy. The visionaries who espoused it were part social reformer, part stadium evangelist, and part a loony brand of what today would be called a dietitian, and they preached physical, moral, and spiritual rejuvenation through the offices of the digestive tract. Their belief that the path to salvation leads through the stomach and comes out in paradise is a faith still alive today in naturopathy, nutritional healing, and the more militant forms of organic-foods store.

But sometimes the fanatic speaks better than he knows. The word "gastrosophy" itself, in one of its renderings, means "the wisdom of the stomach," which to me signifies the deep and visceral fulfillments of coming together and eating and drinking. The stomach knows more than we give it credit for. It's no accident that occasions of note are marked by food—the Thanksgiving dinner, the wedding banquet, the birthday cake. Some very old written texts, many of which are versions of even older oral narratives, communicate this same wisdom in descriptions of feasts and prodigal returns, in accounts of pilgrims on a journey or two travelers on the road sharing a meal. It may well be the most ancient and symbolically resonant form of communal participation, satisfying our human nature as it serves our animal one.

I learned rather recently about a mnemonic device, a technique for remembering things, called the "method of loci," which dates to classical antiquity. I was embarrassed to be unfamiliar with it since I received four years of a fairly traditional liberal arts education at the hands of the Jesuits, and something like this is right up their alley. Then again, it could have been one of those things they mentioned when I wasn't listening. The original purpose of this "method of places" was to help orators memorize long and sometimes complicated speeches. Taught for centuries, it came to be known in the Middle Ages as the "palace of memory." The practice, at least in one of its forms, involved visualizing a familiar building and calling to mind each of its rooms, individually and in detail. You then broke the speech down into small sections, began walking through this building, and, by symbolic association or some other means, attached a mental image of each section of the oration to a particular room. To recall the speech, you returned in your mind to the building, walked its rooms again in the original order, viewed the images you had placed in each, and so retrieved the ideas behind them in the correct sequence. I actually gave this a try and had little success, though I may not have been doing it right. On my return trip to the building, I couldn't remember which door I'd come in or where I'd left my car keys. A lot of mental houses are like this.

In the end, however, the memory palace interested me less for its mnemonic uses than for its premise—that recollection has a spatial quality—and for its intuitively familiar connection between a house and memory. They function as figurative representations of each other. Memory forms our most private domestic space, the architecture of our own past, with its hearth, warm rooms and cold ones, vaults of treasure and those place where we just toss our junk, and perhaps its torture chambers. Certain rooms are well maintained and others neglected into forgottenness; a few no longer exist except in the stories told about them. Some of the furnishings are bright and new, others worn or broken and cobbled back together in serviceable misrememberings. It contains abandoned home-repair projects, gifts from other people, things we inherited, and stuff we made ourselves, well or badly. But mentally, it is the place we call home, held together by the narrative of a life. Conversely, a house is an archive of memory, a history of its occupants and their occupation. The scratch on the floor when movers brought in the new piano, the scorch on the fireplace brick from that New Year's Eve that got a little out of hand, the dining room table passed down through four generations surrounded by brand-new chairs, a great-aunt's Niagara Falls 1916 souvenir plate on a shelf next to last June's graduation picture—all these artifacts of living exist simultaneously, just as today's recollection of a story told last year about the events of a decade ago bring all three of those times into the present.

The philosopher Gaston Bachelard celebrated this conjunction between house and memory and explored, at least insofar as I understand him, domestic spaces as the repository—literal, imaginative, and poetic, as he calls it—of associations and rememberings. "Space," he writes, "is compressed time. That is what space is for." And this seems to me exactly so, at least insofar as I understood him. He has much more to say on the subject, but it is thick and rugged going, and I don't have a compass or the right kind of shoes, which is probably for the best anyway. But the compression he speaks of explains why I can remember vividly a thousand things that have happened in this house on the benches yet at the same time cannot fix dates to them or sometimes even place them in chronological order. Everything is there at once, everything talking to everything else.

A house is not just a figure of speech, but it is partly that. A dwelling place is a metaphor—a metonym, really—the container for all that has played out in its spaces. It is filled with a great many of the things comprehended by the verb "to live." The furniture is continually rearranged and alterations made in accordance with what, at any point, seems better to tell the story of that living. Long ago, a friend who was something of an expert in the Homeric epics told me that the whole of the *Iliad*, its characters and their motives, the plot and politics, could be understood only by fully appreciating the ancient Greek word *oikos*; it formed the axle around which the great tale revolved. Though usually translated as "house" or "household," it lacks a modern equivalent, and referred not only to the physical structure but to the immediate family that lived there, the clan, the servants, the domestic arrangements and dynamics, and even to its public personality or identity. As others have pointed out, the concept is probably best understood now through the more familiar word to which it has given rise, "ecology." A house is a web of relationships, a communication among people, spaces, artifacts, memory, and imagination—both a habitat and an inhabitable organism, though perhaps these are the same thing.

4

Montana 59729

Oh wad some power the giftie gie us,
To see oursels as others see us!
It wad frae monie a blunder free us,
An' foolish notion.
—Robert Burns, "To a Louse"

Sitting by the window in a diner fronting the short stretch of Highway 287 that widens into the few hundred yards of Main Street, you get a pretty fair view of how the summer unfolds, day after day, in Ennis, Montana, 59729.

Around eight in the morning, give or take, the fly shops across the street begin to bustle with the rituals of the fishing trade. Guides in shorts and sandals, sunglasses dangling from cords around their necks or pivoted stylishly upward atop their baseball caps, shake hands with today's responsibilities, some of them already wadered up, eager to get going or to impress the guide with their initiative. They wander in and out of the shops, buying flies, licenses, sunscreen. A couple of clients haul gear from the trunk of a car and pass it to their guide, who walks along the trailer frame and climbs around the boat, stowing bags and rod tubes, checking straps and drain plugs with a hint of showmanship that announces that he is a man thoroughly at home with his equipment. His anglers look on admiringly. They all chat for a few minutes, reading one another, trying to get a preliminary sense of how the day will shape up, as a fishing experience and otherwise. The guide leans against the boat gunnel with relaxed authority, talking and gesturing in the manner of one accustomed to being a temporary professional friend. The clients stand with hands in pockets, attentive and nodding. One of them produces a new reel or box of flies he tied in hopes of approval; another drops into pantomime, fighting an imaginary trout on an invisible rod, a fishing story to establish his credentials and confirm that he's not just another sport but a guy who actually fishes. When this bunch leaves, another pulls in to take its place.

All the while, rigs pulling drift boats or rafts come and go in both directions. A ramshackle flatbed rattles by with a loose load of irrigation pipe. Dually pickups tow stock trailers that shed bits of hay and animal smell as they pass by, the drivers in Massey Ferguson caps occasionally waving to someone on the sidewalk. You see mostly business traffic at this hour, the business of play or the business of work. The occasional RV battleship, emblazoned by the manufacturer with an accidentally candid name—"Intruder" or "Interloper"—lumbers awkwardly through town on its way to Yellowstone Park but seldom stops, since Main Street offers few places spacious enough to beach such whales. All of this passes by at the unimpeded pace possible in a place without a single traffic light.

The tourists start to show up an hour or two later. Some of them are day-trippers on their way to somewhere else who've stopped to stroll the sidewalks for an hour since the place has an inviting, if modestly scaled charm. Others have come to stay for a while, doing whatever people who don't fish do instead. A fair number of both types, like the couple across the street, appear to have recently auditioned for a western-wear ad. He shows off a Stetson and expensive boots, a silver belt buckle the size of a turkey platter cinched against an alderman's girth, and an ample booty waging war on the straining stitches of a crisp new pair of Wranglers. She displays the ruffle, flounce, and hint of lace, the beaded fringe and leather-trim that, according to the Writer, are the essence of ranch-skank couture. Being from Phoenix, she knows. The two of them window-shop a small handful of galleries and antiques places that began cropping up here some years back and specialize in indiscriminately western-themed merchandise: Navajo-style jewelry, regional books, ranch implements from a former age, faux-Hopi pottery, old gold pans, new cowboy hats, rustic furniture, and so forth, often jumbled together with a carelessness that rewards scrutiny. You might, for instance, find an oil painting of a Lakota tipi encampment along a cottonwood-lined stream, all very serene and romantically stylized; placed next to it, with no visible sign of irony, is a cast bronze of some guy on a galloping horse gunning down a buffalo.

It will continue like this for much of the day, out-of-towners walking the short strip of Main Street, looking for retail stimulation, an ATM, or, unsuccessfully, a Starbucks. Later in the afternoon, the guides return and drop off their clients with handshakes all around, high fives and heavy tips if it's been a good day, and the saloons across from the pharmacy begin to shoulder the weight. The sound of laughter and talk stirred together with jukebox music spills out onto the sidewalk whenever someone opens a door, a little louder each time as the evening goes on, which it often does until the tiny hours of the morning.

Over the years, bit by bit, Main Street has undergone the kind of rustic architectural makeover that's become increasingly common in the West—not the scrupulous replica of a historical Wild West town, which would appall most people, but more like an artist's rendition of one. The shop fronts have been face-lifted and interiors redesigned to conform to the nostalgic image of a past that quite probably had little objective reality to begin with. In Ennis, none of this has been undertaken with a movie-set sense of period reproduction—no wooden sidewalks or hitching posts, no blacksmith shop selling forged-iron backscratchers, no gunfights staged every afternoon for the kids. Some of the shop fronts rise in Old West façades with signs that suggest a territorial pedigree—"The Old Madison Valley Trading Company and Mercantile Shoppe," and so on—painted in slab-serifed, ornamental typefaces. But the tentacles of Disney have not yet reached here and transformed Ennis into a parody of itself; nor does it look like a community with a public face entirely orchestrated by the chamber of commerce. It presents mainly the aspect of a regular small town spruced up a bit here and there in an effort to accommodate the expectations of people whose idea of the West comes largely from Louis L'Amour and so put them in a spendable mood. And that seems fair.

Ennis, however, comes by its frontier-flavored credentials honestly. It was homesteaded as a trading post near the end of the Civil War when prospectors struck gold nearby, and after the strike played out, a few years later, it became a cattle town. But the country around Ennis is authentically western in the more complex, contemporary sense as well. It embodies the kind of tensions surfacing throughout range country in the Rockies: between ranching and real estate, the environmental common weal and a long-held sanctity of private property, those who wish to leave water in rivers and those who don't, an older vision of rural life and encroaching development, local people and newcomers. The town shows signs of an agricultural economy yielding to one fueled by the leisure, desires, and credit cards of temporary visitors. And the response, if not uncommon, is ironic nevertheless—the New West coping with the pressures of modernity by evoking the image of an Old West that was in large part responsible for creating those pressures in the first place. This kind of feedback loop does not appear to have a natural stopping point.

In Ennis, the scale of change, though still comparatively small, is headed inexorably in the direction of more and more people. But despite the intermittent carpet bombing of five-acre ranchettes over the surrounding landscape, the town is as yet a long way from becoming Bozemanized, Aspenated, or Jackson Holed out of existence. Step a half block off Main Street in any direction and you end up in someone's backyard. It doesn't have the feel of a conventional tourist destination, in part because it is a specialized one, among a handful of authentic trout towns scattered around the country, mostly in the West. You don't run across them often because the conditions indispensable to a true trout town occur only rarely. First, the fishing must be good enough and the trout water sufficiently plentiful to draw a critical mass of anglers—that is, one with a density both annually reliable and acceptably profitable. And second, the town itself must be small enough and the influx of visiting fishermen large enough that the local economy and public life of the place are, to a perceptible extent, given over to angling-related matters.

As Main Street denotes the physical center of the place, trout fishing defines its conceptual nucleus. Every summer, for instance, a local conservation organization raffles off a brand-new drift boat. Fitted with a sign advertising its intentions, the boat will sit in front of a local motel for a few days, then suddenly materialize one morning in front of the bank, where it stays for a few more, and then turn up in a parking lot at the edge of town, as though through some mysterious agency it moves itself around, trolling for donations. In a more permanent homage to angling, civic pride has erected a nine-foot-tall metal sculpture of a fly fisherman playing a proportionately oversized fish, a stout wire line connecting the tip of a permanently arced rod to the lip of a perpetually jumping trout some yards away. This monument is tellingly sited—not in a public park or in front of the library but in a triangular plot of grass formed by the Y-shaped intersection of the two busiest roads in town. In rural New England, it would probably showcase a Revolutionary War cannon and commemorative plaque; in the Midwest, a hale welcome from the Rotary Club or a larger-than-life concrete Holstein. Here, you find a guy fishing in traffic, and doing fairly well, I might add—the iconic representation of a place where trout are both a business and an atmospheric condition. About one thousand people live in Ennis, but during the course of a summer, tens of thousands pass through, a great many of them carrying fly rods. To a significant extent, both directly and indirectly, the town revolves around fishing and rivers in ways that visiting anglers have come to depend on. Whether this finally reduces to a form of parasitism or resolves to a type of symbiosis depends, as always, on how people behave.

I am endlessly mystified by the good humor the people of Ennis maintain in the face of the annual multitudes, those of us at the ranch certainly included, who crowd them off their home water and into working overtime, consume a lot of space in a little town, and generally use up the air. I doubt that under the same circumstances I could summon up much in the way of cordiality, having a rather low tolerance for people like myself. But I can't recall one instance in the past twenty years of any dealings in town that were other than pleasantly professional at the least and more often genuinely genial, though it pays not to press things too far. People have their limits, and you are wise not to discover them. Any unpleasantness, and that usually of a minor and short-lived sort, is more likely to take place on the river and rarely involves people from town; they have day jobs. And I suspect that the prevailing temper of a trout-town clientele especially taxes their equanimity. A simple subcategory of tourist, the visiting angler is apt to regard his destination in the one-dimensional, even caricatured, fashion of the transient. He sees through a fish-eye lens that produces its several distortions, beginning with the unconscious assumption that because he revels in the buoyancy of a holiday mood, everyone else—the gas-station attendant, the stock boy at the grocery store, the receptionist at the clinic—automatically wishes to share in his ebullient spirits and participate in the elated, zero-gravity space walk of his own unfettered leisure. How could they not?

To be fair, if this impulse toward indiscriminate goodwill sometimes expresses itself as an exaggerated affability or inappropriate gregariousness, it nonetheless signifies a sincere attempt to register pleasure and appreciation at being in the place, even as it fails to recognize that the locals may not regard their town as quite the picturesque novelty you do. And even a well-meaning gesture, clumsily expressed, risks misinterpretation. Talking once with a woman who worked in a restaurant, I happened to remark on how lucky she was to live in a place as beautiful as the Madison Valley, with the mountains, and the gigantic sky, and a river running through it, and so forth. She looked at me as though I'd just confessed surprise that people way out here speak English. "Luck," she said in a tone of mild offense, "had very little to do with it." Almost universally, though, a visitor finds his good intentions returned in kind. Still, it must get tiresome to be surrounded all day by the relentless joviality of people at play and, in varying degrees, oblivious to the fact that you are not.

In Ennis, as in all places, you do run across those socially underqualified embarrassments who make you cringe for your species: the overly loud and overbearing, the rude and the invasively chummy, the urban parochials who complain about all the rudiments of survival that cannot be had in town— today's *Wall Street Journal*, enough bars on their cell phones, a masseuse, covered parking, someone to launder the dog. But even these people do not seem especially numerous, though the locals may well dispute this. I've never heard them speak to the subject—a testimony to excellent manners, though doubtless they talk of it among themselves. But I don't believe I've ever met a resident of the town who confessed to, or showed visible signs of, being worked up, burned out, or soured by the summer crowd, nor have I ever sensed a subcurrent of antipathy or resentment. Maybe you learn to disguise it or just figure out how to pace yourself for the long season. But somehow, they manage an enduring sense of humor and ease.

It is less clear why. I'm familiar with the explanations premised on economic gratitude—people behave graciously because they want or need your money. And this probably holds true for a few; the summer months here serve the same retail function as Christmas at the mall. But this argument has, at best, a simulated plausibility. I do not subscribe much to trickle-down theories; they imply a principle of economic gravity that is routinely defied in the physics of wealth. This kind of seasonal cash flow ripples rather unevenly through a locality, and in my experience, a rising tide mainly lifts yachts and pirate ships. Most of the local people, at least the ones you transact with day to day, pilot a more workmanlike craft. While even a smallish business may make its nut during the tourist season, individual people, as a rule, do not. I suppose you might chalk up the prevailing goodwill to the general small-town friendliness people always talk about, though this doesn't really explain much.

I seldom spend a great deal of time in Ennis, often just long enough to pick up a few necessities, a spool of tippet or yet another bottle of floatant to replace one the Mechanic has borrowed and instantly misplaced. But fishing brings us through with a convenient regularity for this sort of thing, and I end up stopping fairly often. Then, too, I find Ennis a perfectly agreeable place and have come to regard its idiosyncrasies with affection, as charming quirks rather than shortcomings; extreme leisure promotes an expansive view of things. Navigating the town, as you have probably surmised, poses no great hardship, there being so little of it, and running a few errands does not require much time or effort. Ennis doesn't have one of everything and generally offers only one of what it does have—one grocery store; one hardware store; one pharmacy; one phone-booth-sized drive-through espresso hut that, for a short time, was appetizingly named The Brown Gargle, until the owner either sold out or recovered his senses; one barbershop; one laundromat; one movie theater; and so forth. However contrary it runs to the American delirium for "freedom of choice"—a liberty, according to recent polls, that quite a number of my countrymen believe is constitutionally enshrined—this uncomplicated retail landscape makes negotiating the consumer world refreshingly efficient. The town has, nevertheless, supplied itself with two or more of certain essentials—mainly places to eat, places to drink, and fly shops—and one is always grateful to find these in multiples. Out of a sense of fair play and strict neutrality in local matters, we divide our custom more or less evenly among them. And all of these places fit comfortably within the circumference of one zip code and one area code, with, I suspect, considerable room left over.

Most often, the need for provisions brings us to Ennis; keeping ten or twelve people reasonably well fed every day requires a constant renewal of supplies unless you are uncommonly well organized, which we are commonly not. After a routine stop at the aforementioned grocery, a large building for some reason kept cold enough to host a penguin-breeding program, we head to the one butcher shop in town. This transcendent palace of raw protein would do credit to a city fifty times larger, and so comes as a surprise in a place of this size. They make a good sausage on the premises, a highly respectable andouille in particular; trim meat in the way God intended; and size the cuts, steaks particularly, in a manner that suggests that cleaver strokes are discouraged as a matter of house policy. The lengthy refrigerated counter of possibilities often occupies us for quite a while; sometimes, the Cook and the Mechanic must be removed by force.

If conditions in the basement back at the ranch have grown sufficiently dire, we will also swing by the local disposal site on the edge of town. There, we add our contribution to what sanitation professionals call the "waste stream," which conjures up some nasty mental images, though I suppose it captures the basic idea pretty accurately. Sometimes, I'll linger for a bit. I'm not inordinately fond of dumps, and I have never made a special trip just to look one over. But when there, I find them weirdly compelling for reasons I can't quite explain—all that stuff, so visually overwhelming in the details and arresting as a collective. If nothing else, a dump testifies unambiguously to the warped priorities in a country where the goods contained may cost less than their phenomenally redundant containers; where the disposable packaging lasts longer than the automobiles; where the highest attainable virtue in food products is infinite shelf life, while that of consumer durables is instant obsolescence or total breakdown the moment the warranty expires, which one must at least admit takes some clever engineering.

The dump in Ennis—which, I don't mind saying, is my favorite dump—houses a recycling operation that, while small and rather primitive by some standards, soldiers on bravely for the cause. A couple of Dumpsters accumulate the bulk of what comes in, mostly plastic garbage bags that could hold something of interest, though I'm unwilling to invest what it takes to find out, and the Painter would not stand for it anyway. The most intriguing part of the site, however, consists of a small area set off to one side of the main show and informally reserved for stuff people feel a little guilty about just throwing out. Instead they consign it to this staging area of unresolved fates where outdated computer monitors, a pair of wobbly end tables, a dented barbecue grill, TV trays, an old hot tub, a leaky pickup-truck canopy, an exhausted love seat, and that kind of thing wait for a taker. Beyond the simple and practical thrift of it, I admire a certain subversiveness in this consumer-to-consumer loop that refuses to engage the wheels of conventional commerce in the transfer of commodities. It has a communal and egalitarian feel, not only because everything's free but because it represents a shared perception of the delicate distinction between junk and garbage. If I happen to run to the dump with the Bodhi, we will sometimes look over these items, not with the intention of taking anything back but just to see what has come and gone and remained since the last trip, what sells and what's tough to move. Such artifacts speak to the everyday matters of locality. They hint at the invisible lives that take place beyond the transactions of Main Street, lives quite probably like your own. You never really think to imagine them, but if you should, they will remind you that the town is not a stage set peopled with extras in a fly-fishing movie starring you. Usually, though, I just pitch the trash and leave.

For the angling contingent at the ranch, the only other predictably regular stop in town comes at one or more of the fly shops. The Mechanic in particular favors these trips as occasions to try to pry loose some usable information from the counter help, most of whom are seasonal and young but enforce the feeling nevertheless that you are dealing with specialists. Surprisingly, he sometimes succeeds, maybe because he never pretends to be a better fisherman than he actually is, which must seem refreshing in a fly shop. The Cook and I leave this kind of reconnaissance to him, since we have small expectations of acquiring much intelligence that you might categorize as "true." In a fly shop, the fishing is almost universally good, at least according to the reports posted daily on a large whiteboard outside. These always bring to mind a parody I once read of the headlines in sensationalized, grocery-store tabloids: "Man Unhurt as Gas Stove Fails to Explode!" The fishing board instills in me the same sense of wonder and surprise: action on the river is "very good to excellent"—again today! What luck! I don't attribute this, or at least most of it, to deception for profit, partly because fly shops communicate in the idiom of expectancy, a dialect of optimism that comes from a more generous parallel universe. When shop people speak of river conditions, of sizes or numbers of trout, of the density and duration of hatches, it's as though they put everything in dog years, much like the statements handed down annually by the federal-budget fairy. You need to have some idea of the conversion factor in order to get the gist of it.

The only deliberate misrepresentations in a fly shop occur when the fishing turns truly terrible—or "fair to good," as the board outside candidly admits. You may have gathered this firsthand, having fished the river hard for three or four straight days with precious few trout to show for it and not a single encouraging sign. You believe you know the score. But every angler who experiences bad fishing fears, above all else, that he's the only one who's experiencing it. Such insecurities make easy prey, and when some luckless angler steps into a shop and asks about the fishing, secretly seeking reassurance that things are tough all over, he seldom meets with an altogether honest answer: No one's doing any good, you can't do much about it, don't worry, things will change. The shop personnel have an image to burnish, and while they won't actually lie, they will engineer responses scrupulously calibrated to mislead: "Well, the guys who know how can get 'em." This might be true, but only in the sense of being a definition. And it leaves the unfortunate customer with the impression that (a) not getting 'em is all his fault, (b) he is not a guy who knows how, (c) they are, and (d) he has put himself at their mercy. At this point, he's arrived on familiar ground involving a few dozen new flies, some special nonsnagging split shot, a double handful of strike indicators, and a credit card. In the end, this may not be a bad thing. He didn't really buy flies as much as he bought confidence, a commodity not easily obtained under most circumstances. Without it, he might not get back on the water, which is precisely what he needs to do to catch fish. And at worst, I suppose, it merely entertains the shop guys and helps keep them sane as they get asked the same questions several dozen times an hour, day after day, over the course of a long season.

As that season goes on and the valley fills up, more and more with each successive summer, and even the very anglers who are filling it up start to grumble about all the tourists, you begin to question seriously how the whole thing feels to the people who actually live here. I sometimes try to imagine what it would be like to have my home space overrun each summer just when I'd like to be on the water myself but can't find any room. I wonder how I would react to having the tenderloin of my year carved up and served to strangers who showed up just in time for dinner and will leave right after dessert, while I am working extra hours in the kitchen. I suppose that the year here, as it does everywhere, would still contain those blessed but short intervals that you wish lasted longer—early summer when the weather turns pleasant and the locals still outnumber the tourists, and then again in fall when the great balloon of people deflates. But the summer itself would perhaps leave one feeling a little cheated. Under the circumstances, I would probably regard the fishing multitudes with some indignation, as trespassers of a sort—not on the river, which belongs to everyone, most of whom apparently visit it every year, but into the precincts of my life.

I know virtually no one at all in Ennis but have from time to time broached the subject with checkout clerks, bartenders, and the guys in an auto parts store I was forced to frequent with depressing regularity one summer, trying to squeeze an extra year out of the worst car I ever owned.

I've tried to determine how they view the onslaught of people into the space of their lives during what I at least assumed were the best months of the year. But they either parried my questions or returned a noncommittal shrug that said, "It's just the way the things are," an unavoidable subplot in whatever narrative they have invented for themselves. I've never gotten far with these inquiries, and to press the matter might only compound the sense of intrusiveness I cannot help but think they already feel, because I would feel it myself—an ungenerous gauge that quite probably does the people in town an injustice.

Speculating about the lives of local residents inevitably leads me to envision what it might be like to be one of them and live here myself, a common enough fantasy where trout towns and visiting anglers are concerned. But hypothetically trying on a place like this for size quickly brings you face to face with a deficiency of any functional information, your concrete experience being confined to a laughably small and unrepresentative fraction of the whole. You imagine, for instance, that the winters can be long and brutal, but exactly how long they last and the specific shape of that brutality never come sharply into focus. (I did spend a few days here one winter; the temperature hit sixty-five degrees, the wind remained dead calm, and I had excellent fishing. The locals advised me not to read too much into this.) And so deprived of any real material to work with, you keep circling back to what you already know, and your attempts to reconstruct, rationally and accurately, the texture of daily life as a resident here devolve into implausible, indefinitely extended extrapolations of the familiar—in my mental image, it is always summer, grasshoppers are always about, and I am always fishing, with no visible means of support. Even in the most wishful of moods, I can sniff this out for a fraud. And if my conjectures have not carried me very far in picturing myself here, they've brought me no distance at all in seeing through the eyes of the local residents or understanding how they view the summer invasion. To envision other people's lives means something rather different than merely projecting yourself into their circumstances, though the two often get confused. Sympathetic imagination and narcissism never lie far apart.

In the end I am only a tourist, and tourists in a trout town fall into one of two operative categories: those who fish and those who do not. Part of what defines a trout town in the first place is that nearly everybody assumes you're one of the former, and this statistically safe supposition reverberates its small consequences outward into the local life. For one thing, most of the people in town can talk a little fishing. Even those who don't fish inevitably absorb some knowledge of the river and the trout, just as one acquires the rudiments of a foreign language by living among people who speak it. Practically no one, for instance, needs an explanation of how fly fishing differs from bait fishing; they may not understand why we prefer it, but they recognize that we do. Even people who don't care one way or the other usually know how the river's been fishing, and just about everyone has a working familiarity with anglers even if they do not comprehend them. Eccentric behaviors pass without comment: someone ordering a porterhouse and a vodka martini at ten A.M. or a short stack and coffee just before midnight; people in waders sitting on bar stools; boots dangling by their laces from motel doorknobs, the room inside a catastrophe of tackle and fly-tying gear; the funny hats everyone's wearing. All of this goes unquestioned because people already know the answer from long acquaintance with the angler's irregular hours and semioccult habits.

In my experience, the people in a trout town see you primarily, and perhaps exclusively, as a fly fisherman because they have no particular need to see you as anything else. I suppose one might object to this as categorical and reductive, but then in the course of ordinary life we are often enough regarded in ways that reduce us to considerably less: party of the first part; principal taxpayer; third office on the left; and a host of alphanumeric selves. And it is certainly more gratifying to be cast in terms of something you love rather than some duty you perform or obligation you fulfill. Out of curiosity or courtesy, people in town might ask where you've come from, but the baggage of that place remains discreetly unopened. Each has in the eyes of the other a paradoxical kind of public presence, one both generically familiar and comfortably anonymous. In this sense, a trout town represents a kind of tacit understanding. A general goodwill prevails, but you stay removed from the rivalries, allegiances, and entanglements that can be far more complicated in a small town than in a city; the locals, in turn, remain detached from the rest of who you are. Instead, you agree to meet in a separate territory defined by the rivers and fishing that exists in the overlap of your separate orbits. It is a mutually created space, a kind of inhabitable narrative of its own told at the intersection of work and leisure, of the domestic and the wild. All in all, this seems a rather good deal for everyone.

5

To Steal a March

When in Rome, do Rome.
— Mississippi John Hurt

ALTHOUGH I HARBOR NO SPECIAL ILL WILL TOWARD MY FELLOW MAN, I'D much prefer not to run across him when I'm fishing and have no doubt that my fellow man feels precisely the same way about me. But in peak season a river like the Madison seldom admits such luxury. Each of us laments an excess of others that runs from overabundance on slower days to superabundance the rest of the time. As a rule, whatever develops in the way of impatience or irritation remains largely impersonal, directed less at other fishermen specifically than to the fact of their numbers in general, though a few always manage to confuse a cause for regret with the right to complain and mistake groundless resentment for justified indignation. Everyone here, however, is here just like everyone else, all ticks on the same dog. A surplus of people has already become the defining predicament of the twenty-first century and, in fishing, one not likely to disappear until the last stretch of trout water in America flows off-limits behind the locked and guarded gates of privilege or the last trout goes belly-up from any one of a hundred currently impending causes. In the meantime, you can grouse about the crowds, just not legitimately, and so you try your best to tamp down the annoyance and disappointment you are unentitled to feel at seeing your favorite reaches of water occupied day after day.

Surprisingly little of this has much to do with actually catching fish. A glut of rods on the water, I think, does less harm in this respect than people commonly assume, a bit of a hindrance, certainly, but not a critical impediment. It ultimately bears more on where or when you may fish rather than your chances of success. A great many fishermen float the river, and while the steady procession of boats does entail its demoralizations, it can also be instructive. Constantly on the move, with only one or two fleeting opportunities at any given spot, the drifting angler cherry-picks the water, an approach better calculated to the easy fruit than to the best. More than once, sitting on the bank eating lunch or taking a break, I've kept my eye on a likely piece of water—maybe a tongue of deeper current squeezing between two boulders—and watched until several boats, let us say ten, have come downriver, taken a crack at it, and moved on. On some days, this does not take long.

In my experience, six of these efforts will be doomed from the start, the target missed or the fly drifting unnaturally. Of the remaining four, two attempts will be adequate—the fly close enough but not quite on the money, or on the mark but dragging a little. Of the last two, one will be very good and one perfect. This distribution of results owes partly to matters of skill (novices are well represented on the river), partly to the reality that even good fishermen pooch it now and then, and partly to the psychology of continuing opportunity in which the new water ahead absolves the man in a boat from bringing his best game on every shot. But four casts of the passable-or-better sort scarcely scratch the surface of prime water; moreover, eight of the ten boats are probably pitching identical, or nearly identical, flies. The angler who proceeds with more care and a greater deference to the possibilities will take trout where others have already fished and, often enough, even if they've caught something. Naturally, one would always choose to be the first and only angler at a spot, but on the Madison, at least, other fishermen do not seem to me a major obstacle in that they "compete" with you for trout, and I don't believe they materially reduce the quality of your fishing. But they do diminish the quality of your fishing experience, which, if you value a sense of seclusion and privacy, represents the less desirable alternative.

The obvious, by definition, suggests itself: fish somewhere less crowded. On occasion, we do just that, for southwest Montana and its immediate precincts comprise a generous supply of elsewheres. It's pointless, of course, to seek relief on rivers like the Big Hole, Henrys Fork, those in Yellowstone Park, or any of the other celebrated venues of bumper-to-bumper angling. But every larger river in this mountainous country comes conveniently equipped with several small tributaries that supply it with water, though less than they did in the days prior to industrial-scale irrigation. Some very pleasant fishing can be had on these streams; quiet and comparatively unvisited, they hold respectable numbers of trout, mostly small but well formed, sublimely colored, and usually willing. And we will sometimes set out for one of these little mountain creeks, but always drawn by a change of scenery rather than driven by some frustration that the Madison has become too crowded. In my measure of such things, "too crowded" describes its perpetual condition, and were that to specify a principle of exclusion, we'd never fish the river at all.

Still, we have traveled to the Madison Valley expressly to fish the Madison and so have come to accept the inevitability of other people in the way one accepts a right-hand wind or afternoon hailstorm, as a kind of pervasive human weather that must be abided. It may rain on your expectations, but if the presence of other fishermen ruins your day, the problem should be reckoned yours, not theirs. Every trout stream exacts some type of accommodation—difficulties in getting there, fish that are indifferent or scarce or unforgiving, obstacles of terrain and water, a severe climate, pestilential insects, or enormous expense. Long ago we learned that fishing in the company of others is the particular price of admission to the Madison, the cost of doing Rome.

That having been said, one need not always pay full retail. You cannot eliminate the crowds, but you might minimize their intrusions into your own enjoyment. Over the years, we have adopted various measures to this end, all issuing from a single imperative: when given the choice, choose to flee. In the face of superior numbers or overwhelming firepower, the smart money will concede the game and leave the devil his due. Surrender may not be a particularly ennobling personal response, but it is a proven one and has served me well in managing the persistent and unwanted intrusions of life more generally.

The application of this policy on the Madison is pretty elementary: forfeit the water in those times and places you might ordinarily choose to fish it and withdraw to the nooks of the river and corners of the day that others dismiss as too unpromising or too much trouble. At the risk of pointing out the obvious, should you be seeking "Hot Tips to Escape the Summer Crowds," you may wish to consult a fly-fishing magazine instead, since our approach does not exactly score high marks for originality. On the whole, we are not keen tactical thinkers, and perhaps all I can say on behalf of our strategy is that formulating it occasioned us no great trouble and that it sometimes succeeds. With a little luck, we might outflank the masses for a time and fish a satisfying portion of the day in reasonable solitude. Whether avoiding the popular times and places presents any advantages in the actual catching of trout—a strong but secondary motive of ours—is doubtful. Other anglers fish when and where they do for eminently sensible reasons.

Fly fishing is, among other things, a sport of ironies and occasionally of compensatory ones; our efforts to elude the surplus of other anglers gets some assistance from an unexpected quarter, the very one that in part accounts for the crowds in the first place. The guides that work the river in summer observe a fairly regular routine and put in reasonably predictable, if long hours, typically arriving at the river between eight and ten in the morning and pulling off between three and six. While you find plenty of exceptions, in aggregate their movements and habits show a comfortable consistency and so provide one of life's rare opportunities to avoid what you can see coming.

Our earliest attempts to exploit this behavior centered principally on fishing in the evenings after the guides had punched out and the clients, with a solid and fatiguing day's fishing behind them, had packed it in for the night. But it didn't take long to discover that, having already put in a long and tiring day ourselves, we were about ready to hang it up by sundown, too. You can fish from the dark of the morning to the dark of the night only in short bursts—a long weekend, maybe a week; after that, you start feeling a little strung out and at some point recognize that you're doing it just to do it, not because you're actually having fun. So after a time, the evening fishing settled, or perhaps devolved, into a routine that acceptably negotiated the desires of the spirit with the demands of the flesh. Reluctant to subject the river and ourselves to the second full-scale beating of the day but unwilling to call it quits altogether, we would pack up a car or two just before dusk, drive to the river, and set up camp chairs and a cooler along a guard rail on the edge of a bridge that was, in the evening hours, functionally untraveled. One among us, occasionally two, was nominated to occupy the water immediately below the bridge and fish for the amusement of the rest.

August evenings on the river are unusually agreeable. The air cools quickly after sunset, but the land continues to radiate heat, and from time to time a wayward breeze lifts a billow of earth-warmed air and pours it over you like a wave. It smells of sagebrush and mown alfalfa and the mineral dampness of a trout stream. The elevation of the bridge offers a lovely prospect of the river and an ideal view of the angler below. On a clear night around the full moon, the fishing might go on late, each of us taking a turn with the rod while the rest kibitz from the bridge. We might call out for a change of fly, or a different technique, or should nymphs be involved, raise the cry for ever more split shot, and generally supply encouragement while attempting to persuade the designated angler to use the pattern we would use and fish it as we would fish it, without going to the trouble of doing so ourselves. In this fashion, the armchair anglers, from the comfort of the bleachers, would manipulate their little proxy until it grew too dark to see.

Over the course of a few years, however, these trips began tapering off and eventually came to an end, for a couple of reasons. First and as you might imagine, we didn't actually catch all that much. Five or six spectators parked in chairs, sipping beer, and watching one guy fish the same spot over and over is not exactly a winning formula for nonstop action, satisfying as it might be in other respects. And second, these entertainments suffered interruption rather too often by the appearance of a man sufficiently well-heeled to have acquired substantial acreage bordering the river next to the bridge. He ranched his hobby farm from the cockpit of a late-model Land Rover bearing the license plates of a well-known eastern state. I would like to think, though one can never be certain in these cases, that were I in the driver's seat, I would pass the days in speechless gratitude for whatever blessed fortune brought me a piece of land adjoining some of the best big-fish water on one of the most distinguished trout streams in America. He saw the matter otherwise, from a position that would be fairly described as one burst vessel short of apoplexy, outraged at the mere possibility that someone had violated, was in the process of violating, or would very soon violate one of the several hundred "No Trespassing" signs that ringed his empire.

And so he would show up with depressing frequency, driving up to the bridge at a low and mistrustful speed, as though searching for roadside explosives, and begin his interrogations: How did that guy down there get to the water without crossing his land? Don't you see the land is posted? What are you even doing here on the bridge? I doubt there's an angler alive, at least one with any imagination, who hasn't at some time or other trespassed on posted land or snuck onto private water. But this is—barring exceptional circumstances, of course—largely an adolescent thrill; with age, you grow a little more circumspect, or at least more fearful of getting caught, and we had given it up long ago. Evidently he didn't recognize us from one confrontation to the next and invariably tried to bluff us away, first with suggestions that he owned the streambed itself; then by hazy insinuations that even the bridge had, through an arrangement too complex to detail, been ceded to his control by local authorities; and, failing that, by resorting to what sounded, if not like actual threats, at least like menacing vocalizations. He appeared to believe, in some inarticulable way, that he held jurisdiction not only over his own land but over the river, the bottom, the bridge, and the adjacent lands that belonged to someone else. Ultimately he was powerless to evict us, in his eyes a regrettable injustice of public-access law, which, if properly written, would not only keep people off his land but out of sight of it altogether. None of this appeared to be personal, as he inflicted these imperious tantrums on anyone within earshot. The Cook, especially offended by this belligerence, took to calling him the Hun.

I could never understand what this man feared—perhaps that any small breach in the perimeter of his holdings would culminate in a torchlit mob of the unwashed advancing on the castle to seize his big-screen TV and carry off his women. In any case, he appeared agitated to the point of involuntary twitching that we, that anybody, should enjoy ourselves in a place that properly, if not quite lawfully, belonged to him—a textbook illustration of H. L. Mencken's definition of Puritanism: "the haunting fear that someone, somewhere, may be happy." It was never clear why he chose to torture himself this way, but the Hun spent much of his time behind tinted glass in semiconcealed surveillance, scouring the landscape through expensive binoculars, impatient to enforce claims that were rightfully his and shored up, I have no doubt, by the flying and highly paid buttresses of a crack legal team.

But being compelled to stand our ground repeatedly in these altercations—for such disputes are by no means pointless—succeeded only in draining any pleasure from the occasion, and the evening inevitably reduced to the kind of heated and petty amateur litigiousness into which every small question in America eventually plummets. This was not a part of Montana that we had imagined for ourselves, and so we abandoned the nights at the bridge. For all I know, crushing our wills like this had been the Hun's plan all along.

The logical recourse required no strenuous conceptual leap: instead of staying out late, we began starting out early, rising before dawn to arrive at the ramp well in advance of the guides and, theoretically, get in a day's fishing, or the better part of one, without ever seeing another boat. This plan survived the inconveniences of reality in the way of all theories, incompletely and intermittently, but well enough to have become standard practice for many years now. I have always favored morning fishing anyway. The first hours of light on a river are the most gracious of the day. Cool night air still lingers over the water, and there is seldom any wind. Shadows stretch out as the day uncurls in the yawn of morning sun, and the river is never more quietly spectacular nor the landscape more vividly limned than in that slanting light. Nocturnal creatures wander home, diurnal ones take their place, and there is much to see at the change of shift, as in truth there is at dusk. But the sun sets with a sense of time seeping away, of attenuation and impending conclusion; with dawn, the day just keeps getting bigger, and for several hours the far end of it is quite invisible. The fishing prospects, as yet uncorrupted by the fish, are envisioned through the purities of early-morning hope and its innocent interpretations of the future. At sunrise on a trout stream, every man is an optimist.

The pleasures of a morning can be had on foot as well. Some days we would drive to a ramp at daybreak and wade upriver, indifferent to the boats that would soon put in below us, and still hours away from those that would drift down to us from the next launch point above. As often as not, we set out for a specific section of water—for both practical and selfish reasons, you must forgive me for not identifying it more precisely— that lies somewhere in the river's vast patchwork of islands. Getting there required a bit of a hike, but eventually we would strike the water at the foot of a run perhaps twenty-five feet wide and three times that long, nowhere more than waist-deep. It was one of those inexplicable spots that almost all good trout streams possess, where you might raise a few fish to dry flies even when the rest of the river is quiet as a corpse. From there, we would weave back and forth among the islands, fishing only a few select points, having through trial and error weeded out those ideal-looking places that never produce, which is another enigma shared by all trout streams. In time, we would end up at a pair of pools, Upper Cook's Hole and Lower Cook's, separated by a short, shallow stretch of fast water on an unassuming side channel.

This bit of water, as you might guess, owes its name to the Cook, whom I have known since boyhood. Even early in life, he demonstrated an immoderate penchant for parody and satire, on the one hand, and no patience whatsoever for self-importance or pretentiousness in people, on the other. These have only intensified with the years, the first manufacturing antibodies to combat the second in a kind of psychic immune response that is both rapid and broad-spectrum. He maintains, as Herbert Spencer did, that "the ultimate result of shielding men from the effects of folly is to fill the world with fools." So when it comes to fishing, the Cook has no patience with the kind of vocal showboating that has come much into fashion on the water these days. The angler who connects with a fish and begins whooping in triumph, capering about extravagantly to attract attention, and otherwise behaving like a human exclamation point is an especial burden to him.

In the presence of such a cartoon, he becomes powerless against his own impulses, and I have watched him more than once deliberately hook a small trout, back down the drag to nearly free spool, and reef on the rod to make the reel whine like a little French motor scooter, at which point he stabs a fist repeatedly in the general direction of heaven, yelling "Yeee-haaaah!" Then, in an overstated show of recapturing line, he reels furiously as he dips the rod tip to the water and stares at the offending fisherman, eyes wide and jaw dropped in astonishment. This performance goes on and on, until an eight-inch trout surrenders from sheer bewilderment or one of us demands that he stop. Egalitarian in every respect, the Cook does not even require the target of his contempt to be present. Standing in the front of the drift boat, he will set the hook on a fish and in a parody of the more egregious forms of angling prose, howl, "Eat hot nylon!," then turn to me at the oars and narrate himself in the third person: "*Good Lord, what a fish!* he involuntarily ejaculated."

Anyway, to the point. He holds in particularly high disregard those self-proclaimed experts who, in person, print, or assorted video formats, run on like a leaky toilet of insufferable hubris about their own expertise generally and, specifically, their claims to have "invented" some angling approach or technique that has in fact been well known, widely practiced, or totally obvious for decades or, in some cases, centuries. The Cook's representative example and chief whipping boy for this kind of behavior is the fly tier who works some insignificant modification on a regulation-issue pattern. This innovator might substitute, say, red wire for copper on the body of a midge-pupa imitation that is already thoroughly generic, then announce that he's designed (sometimes "originated" or even "engineered") a groundbreaking new pattern called something like "Willy's Little Squirt," naming his extraordinary child after himself in a pathetic act of self-merchandising.

Such creatures, in the Cook's eyes, beg for burlesque. So if we are out fishing and he should take a particularly nice trout from some piece of water or other, he'll promptly claim to have "discovered" the spot and continue with a hyperbolic, blow-by-blow replay in which only his various superior skills and superhuman reflexes could have prevailed, always ending the account with " . . . which is why I like to call this spot the Cook's Hole." At one point, there were upward of thirty Cook's Holes distributed along as many miles of Madison, though in time, the one-hit wonders and persistent underachievers were demoted, and the number now hovers around a dozen. This has led to some confusion in our discussions of the river—"Wait: Are you talking about the Cook's Hole right above the bridge or the one right above that?"—but with a little contextualizing information, we manage to keep them more or less straight.

Upper and Lower Cook's are probably the best of the lot, though I'd like it on record that, in fact, I discovered them both. But the Cook would hear none of it and overruled me; to name the place stood as a matter of ironic principle with him. From an aerial view, the two pools and the connecting water would look like a slightly drooping bow tie, and the first morning the Cook and I ever came upon them, we took nine or ten very respectable trout, all on top, from this surprisingly smallish water. It has never fished nearly that well since but still remains one of the better spots, always approached with above-average expectancy. And if you get there early enough, you might enjoy a couple of hours in complete solitude.

To evade the crowds by getting on the river at daybreak proved, as I've said, an imperfect solution. For one thing, it suffers somewhat from a deficiency of imagination. Since the practice goes back to the dawn of angling, we often had company, never in prime-time numbers, but in escalating ones as the years passed and getting a jump on the day grew more popular. This had the effect of pushing our own departure time ever earlier, and there is of course a practical limit to retreating in this direction. Even then, we have always fished more slowly than most people and, when drifting, would eventually be overtaken by a string of boats that had pushed off a few hours behind us. From there on out, only a small advantage remained. Most boats fished at roughly the same tempo, and by syncopating our movements, fishing a half step out of pace in the middle spaces between everyone else, we could still find a little privacy. While not exactly angling to the beat of a different drummer, it did have its payoffs, though in the end they were small.

These sunrise starts entailed other compromises, the most serious of which concerned the fishing itself. By midsummer or so, grasshoppers, the angler's darling, have taken the field, and they have much in common with teenage boys: sleeping late, rising into a prolonged and lethargic quasi-wakefulness, and shaking off the torpor to arrive at full consciousness only when the sun is high and the day warm, at which point they become energetically occupied with finding something to eat. Both can also act with astonishing carelessness, and a grasshopper that ends up in the river, through a miscalculated jump, a faulty flight plan, or an act of God, is the stuff of a trout's dreams and so of a fisherman's. These accidents happen a lot in August—just not in the early morning. While there are trout to be had at these hours, the dry-fly artist is apt to go begging, which if you fly-fish, counts, and if you fly-fish Montana, counts a lot. One does not come here to nymph, though admittedly, if you stay long enough you're likely to rethink this idea. In any event, these early mornings circled us back to the inevitable trade-off: giving up some catching to improve the fishing.

Human beings in general seem constituted to want it all, but fishermen believe they can actually get it. The soul of an angler embraces a collection of unquestioned convictions, foremost among them the faith that a trout could take on any cast. Deprive him of that assumption and only a perplexing sense of waste remains. This proposition is followed closely by the belief that every stream possesses not just isolated, clandestine spots here and there, such as Upper Cook's, but extended reaches of uninhabited water—"secret water" is how it often presents itself, however indistinctly, to the imagination. He envisions it as a stretch of river that, for some reason (the fantasy is never very clear on this detail), other anglers overlook, or ignore, or don't know about and where he may fish alone and in peace. (This belief commonly gives rise to the more general supposition that entire streams of this sort exist. Somewhere.) It is fly fishing's version of the sustaining myth that every culture requires.

For a friend who fished with us off and on in the early years, however, this conviction in undiscovered water went well beyond the usual harmless and simple-hearted faith; it transcended even delusional longing to become a core component of his life energy, his own personal plutonium. Nothing, to his mind, could be more self-evidently true than secret water unless it was the parallel certainty that such a place always lies on the far side of significant toil; if you haven't found it, his reasoning went, you haven't searched or suffered hard enough. He was, in short, an enthusiast and a seeker, and but for the grace of God or an accident of circumstances might have ended up on a remote California mountaintop, a cowled zealot bearing the Golden Horn of Oblique Instrumentality in one hand and a shopping bag of negotiable securities in the other, proffering both to a burnished chrome effigy of Harpo Marx, beseeching his curly and vengeful return in the Monstrous Hour That Was Foretold. Instead he turned out to be a fisherman with a thirst for secret water and an inflexible belief in its existence. I had on countless occasions, back home in Oregon, been baited into one or another of his improbable quests, always strongly imagined but poorly conceived, during the course of which all manner of things would befall us except fish. He envisioned these ventures as swift, stealthy, surgical insertions into unvisited water; to "strike like lightning" was his operative description, though we were far more likely to be struck by it, metaphorically speaking, and a few times came scorchingly close in the literal sense. If he did not visit us on the Madison with a scheme already in mind, he contrived one shortly thereafter and pressed it with evangelical fervor, preying coldly on his fellow anglers' predictable vulnerabilities until even the most outrageous proposal began to make a strange sort of sense as you got caught up in the toxic contagion of his plan.

Which is how, after years of being sucker punched by this kind of thing, I found myself one evening at the ranch, having dined to weakness and pliability, succumbing to one of his schemes. The idea, this time, involved drifting a remote and much-neglected side channel alleged to sidle away from the main river so discreetly that few people even knew of its existence and fewer still fished it. The trout there, it went without saying, were on the large side. My friend apparently learned of this water during a conversation with a young fellow who worked at a fly shop in Ennis. That a shop employee would confide this kind of information to a complete stranger—one, I might add, who almost certainly didn't purchase anything—could suggest only a small and suspicious number of possible meanings, and "being the case" was not likely among them. But it presented just the kind of scenario against which my friend was defenseless; the merest hint of secret water jellied him to an aspic of the purest credulity.

According to our instructions, upon approaching a certain easily identified island, we were to keep to the right of it, and at every subsequent split in the river continue bearing in that same direction until we finally reached a right-hand channel that was clearly too small for the boat. At this juncture, stay to the left and the secret water would lie dead ahead. Follow the directions and "you can't," my friend had been assured, "miss it."

But nothing is foolproof to the truly gifted fool. Admitting, at least for the moment, that the channel in question even existed beyond the perversities of an alienated shop slave, there was some discrepancy about the meaning of "clearly too small for the boat." I understood this in the informal and familiar sense—a channel so unmaneuverably narrow and shallow that even an oarsman of substantially diminished capacity would not attempt it. My companion, an engineer, favored a more literal interpretation in which we were to take any right-hand passage that technically exceeded the measured width of the boat (excluding, of course, the thickness of the paint), even should that margin of difference be only millimeters. That his version might well call for the kind of manual encouragement best applied from outside the boat with pry bars and a winch only proved that we were on the right track, since trout always lie in the direction of greatest hardship. Although it was my boat, he happened to be driving at the pivotal instant; at the head of an island that split off just the kind of channel that I felt merited discussion, he angled right, slid down an incline of damp stones, and squeezed us into a sluggish, turbid ditch so uniform in breadth and depth that it had to have been dug by some sort of machine. There was no room to row—the boat already rubbed against both banks—and so we poled with an oar down that scurvy little trench until we at last rejoined the main river again late in the afternoon. To my recollection, neither of us made a cast.

It is pointless to try to explain how, the following summer, I ended up consenting to yet another of these ordeals; you either understand this sort of thing or, like a rational person, do not. Again the mission revolved around an anonymous side channel holding large trout that were seldom fished; again my friend insisted on the reliability of his intelligence as, again, it had come to him through someone at a fly shop.

"What if he's bullshitting you?" I asked.

"What if he's not!" he replied, and then unrolled a large map of the river and traced with his fingertip the water at issue. He roughed out the plan for me and curried his pigeon by stressing, at strategic intervals, that the likelihood of running into other fishermen was absurdly remote. I knew I was being played—it was always that way with him—but had to concede, all in all, that the thing did not look completely impossible, my usual low benchmark for one of his ideas. Historically, my role in these episodes has been that of skeptic, a foil against which my companion may mount his escalating enthusiasms. With this duty in mind, I pointed out that finding the right channel among a complicated maze of others looked to be a crapshoot, but in truth I'd already yielded to the seductions of the document he had produced. Maps have a way of disabling one's mechanisms of natural caution, like some weird form of nerve gas. Their precise and tidy reductions make everything look so convincingly manageable. It is an intrinsic power of abstractions.

"Really, what's the worst that could happen?" he asked offhandedly, intending to put misgivings to rest but in fact echoing the very question I was putting to myself in a less rhetorical fashion. Before I could finalize a short list of possibilities, he gave what appeared to him the obvious answer.

"We miss the channel and fish our way to the next boat ramp," he said, enlisting the kind of logic that one recognizes only later as a clever simulation.

As it turned out, locating the particular side channel we sought proved simple enough to cause me some concern, for at the head of the island that diverted this little waterway stood a stone cairn, constructed just deliberately enough that you would not mistake it for an accidental arrangement of rocks but sufficiently inconspicuous not to advertise itself. My friend hailed this as confirmation beyond dispute that we had arrived at the spot, and I couldn't deny it. But while it was clear what the marker designated, what it signified remained a matter of troubling semiotic ambiguity. I pointed out that it could mean only one of two things: "This Is the Entrance to the Secret Water," in which case it wasn't all that secret, or "This Is the Channel I Was Warning You About."

And so we took it, pushing through its foamy little throat, bobbing over the dark and intriguing gut of a small pool, and grinding our way over a long shoal of gravel below the tailout. From there, the channel veered obliquely away from the main river, a little stream of its own perhaps twenty-five feet wide.

The water held little promise at first and would continue that way for a time until things finally changed and it held none at all. Of course we didn't know this right away; for the moment, the water simply seemed to lack much depth and cover. We had no reason to believe that the situation would not improve; or, rather, we had every reason if we'd only summoned the courage and clear-mindedness to consult our own prior experiences. We rowed on for perhaps half an hour, scanning for fish, waiting for the stream to perk up and show something interesting. Instead, by degrees the water grew shallower and slower. Navigating around the rocks without the resistance of sufficient current meant pushing the boat forward, weaving from bank to bank, and at times even cutting back upstream to find a path around the next obstacle. We continued in this fashion for some long while, and though it was tedious work, at least if you had expected to be fishing instead, I would later look back on it all fondly as the most idyllic portion of the trip and long for its return.

In places, no clear passage presented itself, and the boat would hang up on rocks just beneath the surface. The water continued to shallow, finally reaching a point where one of us was forced from the boat to reduce the draft and walk alongside, then, as the depth decreased further, to affix a line to the bow and pull us downstream. We took turns at this, and while mine always felt longer, I kept silent. Our progress was slow.

It ceased altogether when we rounded a point of land and found two barbed-wire fences, about twelve feet apart, stretched in parallel across the channel. Between them, on a mud-trodden bank, stood the largest Angus bull I ever hope to see—an enormous and forbidding animal with vast cumulonimbus swells of muscle on its neck and forequarters and a torso as big as a steam boiler abutting the great meaty pistons of its rear haunches, between which hung a scrotum the size of a regulation speed bag and farther along the undercarriage, in an image I will carry to the grave, a prodigious erection. There was not another animal in sight. I admit to understanding little about cattle, but I could not conjure up a single scenario in which this might be construed as a good thing, at least for us, though I was more than a little hazy about what it might mean specifically for the immediate future. The bull stood still as stone and spoke only the cryptic language of nostrils—not exactly snorting, more a sort of huffing, each exhalation sending a cloud of flies and flecks of mucus up from its muzzle into the shimmering sunlight. I have never found any evidence of inner life in the bovine face; it does not seem designed to convey much information, and this one in particular gave no clues to intent. He could have been on the brink of stomping us to a crimson paste or, just as plausibly from his appearance, on the verge of a stroke. Knowing that my companion had raised some lesser forms of livestock in his youth, I looked for him to take charge. He yelled authoritatively, waving his arms and issuing various sharp commands and gruff noises, until I began to worry that he might succeed only in aggravating our circumstances. But nothing made an impression one way or the other, and the bull remained unmoved.

We anchored in uncertainty above the upper fence, pondering our options while we waited to see if the bull might just go away on its own, which it did not. At the end of ten or fifteen indecisive minutes, we concluded that our best move was to crouch down in the water on the far side of the boat, making ourselves as small as possible while we maneuvered it slowly and unthreateningly under the barbed wire. We removed our waders in the anticipation of reverting to Plan B, which was swift evacuation by any route possible, figuring that it could take as long as several seconds for the bull to trample the boat to splinters, giving us a vital head start. That the two fences stood only twelve feet apart complicated matters, since at one point the sixteen-foot boat would have to pass beneath both of them simultaneously, causing a brief but tense delay at the moment we were closest to the animal, a distance of no more than three or four yards. The prospect of being confined in a very small cage with a very large bull was uppermost in our thoughts as we moved cautiously, peeking over the gunnel at the animal to keep up with any potential developments on his end. But it all went more or less according to plan, and the instant that final strand of barbed wire scraped across the boat stern, snapped off the transom, and sprang back into place, the world seemed to me remade.

To his enduring credit, the bull, still much inflated, never so much as twitched. Possibly it was blind.

As I have said, I know nothing of the nature of standing beef beyond what appears to me as a phenomenal stupidity, which I presume to be as dangerous in animals as it is in people, or nearly so, and perhaps it is common knowledge in the farming community that bulls habitually behave like fiberglass replicas of themselves. But to have dodged even an imaginary bullet—or "cheated death," as I thought of it at the time—put the day in a serene new light, and we forged on, our spirits much improved, my companion's in particular. According to his theory, secret water is earned through adversity, and he judged from the events of the day so far that we should be just about there. In fact, after a time the channel began deepening little by little until, to our great relief, there was at last enough depth to float the boat again with both of us in it. Either the water had improved or our expectations sufficiently deteriorated, but the channel even began to look a little like a trout stream, still marginal but better than what we'd been seeing. We started to fish under clear skies and a hot sun that promised to get a great deal hotter, switching off on the rod and oars. We covered perhaps half a mile of water and saw nothing except, in the distance, what appeared to be another fence. It looked too low, however, and as we got closer we thought it could be a broken-down fence, or maybe a tree that had fallen across the stream, entertaining one possibility after another, unwilling to accept the truth that dawned as we grew nearer: a diversion dam that spanned the entire channel. We put ashore to investigate, found the structure to be about four feet high, and sat down once again to evaluate our options.

I cannot recall why we rejected the mildly risky, but probably manageable, and certainly most direct approach: pushing the boat over the edge of the dam. I have successfully repressed whatever that decision involved. (In my mental picture of it, the lip of the dam is studded with shards of glass set in concrete and topped with coils of razor wire, but I'm sure this is not right.) Without much left in the way of choices, we set about emptying the boat, removing the anchor and oars, lightening things up as much as possible so we could portage around the obstruction. The boat itself, though not prohibitively heavy—perhaps 250 pounds—was long, wide, and ungainly, particularly for the projected route along a steep, stony embankment choked with sagebrush and tall weeds.

There is no elegant way to accomplish an undertaking of this sort. It proceeded pretty much as you would expect, with a lot of grunting and panting, sweating and swearing, with frequent pauses to assess whether we were making genuine progress or merely pushing ourselves farther into a situation that we would eventually come to regret. It took some little while in the heat of the day, but we finally wrestled the boat up, around, and back down the bank; made three or four more trips to retrieve the gear; then sat down to rest and confront the fact that the channel below the dam contained virtually no water, most of it having been shunted into an irrigation ditch above. The streambed had not diminished in breadth but held mostly just thinnish puddles of water here and there, with nothing like an actual flow of current through them. So we stowed the oars, hitched a rope to the bow, and one of us pulled while the other pushed, with no clear idea of how far we had yet to go, the map having been silent on the matter of the dam.

There is not much variety to speak of in the remainder of this unhappy business. Under a flash point of white-hot sun in an acetylene-blue sky, sopped in perspiration, we urged the boat African Queen–style along what I suppose was technically still a channel. At scattered intervals, there was enough depth to float the boat temporarily, but nowhere did the water actually reach from bank to bank. It was mostly just a lot of wet rocks, an ever-growing number of which bore the white, chalky residue of important substances they'd scraped from the bottom of the boat as we passed over them.

How long we toiled at this I cannot remember—perhaps an eternity or two. At last, we could see a line of trees off in the distance, marking the main river, though it was still some time before we reached it, sweat-soaked and wrung out. My companion and I collapsed on the bank in exhaustion and gratitude.

"I told you we'd have the place to ourselves" was all he said.

It is an old truism that the best fishing takes place in spaces of transition, on the edges between current and obstruction, shallow and deep, warm and cool, fast and slow, day and night. For someone who seeks solitude—not just on the Madison but quite possibly on any river in the twenty-first century—the best fishing may lie at the edge of someone else's, just beyond the margins of routine times and everyday places. Often, great numbers of trout do not live out there, and you may well sacrifice some catching if you go. I suppose you could regard it as a kind of angling by negation, in which other people are allowed to dictate the terms of your fishing.

But the whole aim is to transpose the customary priorities. It requires certain ingenuities to fashion a space beyond the perimeter of the ordinary, a temporary zone of sovereignty over your own circumstances. In this sense, you invent for yourself a form of fishing; it is a way of creating something, as you might a story or a painting, and possibly for some of the same reasons. You make compromises, certainly, but it's worth bearing in mind that whatever is created or imagined takes shape in part through the forgoing of possibilities, the filtering of choices, and all the forfeitures that leave behind the raw materials from which a thing of value might be fashioned.

Fly fishing of course cannot be called, in any important construction of the term, an "art." It is only a medium.

6

POSTCARDS OF THE HANGING

> For each man kills the thing he loves . . .
> —Oscar Wilde, "The Ballad of Reading Gaol"

AT ONE EDGE OF THE RANCH SITS THE ORIGINAL HOMESTEADER'S CABIN, a compact and unornamented structure built a century ago of hewn logs now weathered to silver-gray and split with age. No one has lived in it for decades. The antiquated electric meter rusting on an outside wall dates from the early 1920s; an asphalt roof, cracked and sloughing, does not appear a great deal newer; at some point, the outside walls were rechinked with fresh cement, which has since loosened and crumbled. The house sags in places and lists a bit at one end, and broken bricks have fallen from the chimney. Yet this footprint of settlement, someone's small claim to a patch of place, remains.

Nothing indicates why these particular homesteaders settled here, pushed out, maybe, by the transatlantic waves of people arriving in the East at the turn of the century, or maybe part of that wave themselves, looking for a new start or a little piece of paradise. From all appearances, they came to stay. There are signs of hopeful domestic intention in a pair of lilac bushes planted out front and, growing next to them, a rosebush—not the kind of rose you see today that looks as though it was designed by an ad agency and carved from a block of lipstick; rather, an older cultivar, not wild but not yet with all the wildness bred out of it. And eleven children, I've been told, were born to the original occupants. Looking at the cabin, you'd think it impossible for so many people to live in such close quarters. Though not a large space, nor one that elaborates the story of its habitation, it summarizes much.

Other homesteaders of the nonnative sort: cattle, horses, cheatgrass, leafy spurge, hound's-tongue, spotted knapweed, hawkweed, yellow toadflax, purple loosestrife, common tansy, carp, brook and brown and rainbow trout, New Zealand mud snails, whirling disease, and scores of others that were brought here, left here, hitchhiked here, or otherwise found their way here to overcrowd, overcome, outcompete, displace, or exterminate indigenous populations. For settlers, ranchers, miners, loggers, developers, and even its legendary vigilantes, Montana has been an opportunity to create a world, to fashion a narrative about what matters to them. Some stories, though, have better endings than others.

If the twenty counties surrounding Yellowstone Park, including those in southwest Montana, were consolidated into a single state, it would be one of the fastest growing in the country. The residential population of the Madison Valley alone is projected to increase by over a third in a single five-year window, a figure that excludes the growth in seasonal and recreational ownership. There has been talk of an improved road from Ennis over the Madison Range to the ski slopes on the east side, and the mere thought of accommodating the winter tourists is already causing a pleasant stirring in the trousers of the real-estate and development interests.

The machine is in motion and a hard thing to stop, presuming you want to stop it in the first place. Some don't, some do, and some do but wonder whether they can afford the trade-off. Do you sell five hundred acres of rangeland, salt away the proceeds to retire on, and feel bad about it? Do you hang on to the land and work a ranch that's barely making it?

Parts of Montana already show signs of tumbling down the chute that ends up in places like Aspen, where luxury real estate has so inflated land values that millionaires are forced out by billionaires, which is hardly a consolation to the local people who can no longer afford to live in the towns where they grew up. Those who do stay form what is discreetly termed the "service sector" and are housed in what amounts to subsidized barracks. Having the help close by is such a convenience.

The young look at all of this and, rightly sensing no future, leave for somewhere else.

I'm hardly the first to point this out: the more people who move to Montana for all the reasons that people move here, the less reason there is to come. When pitchmen for development hawk "plenty of elbow room," naturally what you get is plenty more elbows. But the bar of expectation continually drops. Refugees from both coasts are pleasantly surprised by how few people live here, how less congested it is than home, how inexpensive to bring someone in to have things done. Then they set about re-creating exactly the kind of place they couldn't wait to leave.

Montana is moving at the speed of money. Subdivisions spring up in what is for all purposes the beautiful middle of nowhere, with insufficient infrastructure to support them. Lincoln Log starter castles and custom châteaus disfigure the viewshed, while miles of subterranean sprinkler systems bleed the aquifer to transfuse manicured lawns and exotic ornamentals in arid soil. Scaled to dominate the land, the worst of these places are grotesquely excessive, as though the influx of wealth, overstimulated with what it could buy here and intoxicated with how much, threw up on Montana. The prophets of development extol the profits of development and vend a gospel of growth that threatens to transform localities with a lethal makeover, like that of the TV evangelist's dutiful wife, obligingly primped and painted, who slowly dies of mascara poisoning.

The self-appointed kleptocrats of the American West, privateers who have persuaded themselves that if they do not own every last little bit, they have nothing at all, nod in grave agreement: with so many people wishing to use them, public waters are far too profitable to be left to the public. It is imperative that the rivers and their trout be put into the hands of those who can best realize their market potential. Barbed-wire fences are strung illegally across rivers, and access at public rights-of-way is illegally obstructed, illegally impeding or preventing the recreational use of waterways by ordinary people, those regrettable inconveniences who actually own the rivers.

It reaches back to national beginnings, this perverse equation: being able to afford more means being entitled to more, including the wherewithal to get it. The "Roman qualities of America overwhelm me," writes John Fowles, "everything based on power, on mean gold rather than the golden mean. America is in a way the inability to think of gold metaphorically." As Wall Street insists on redundantly proving, no amount of money can raise some people above the ethical poverty line. To point out a patrician contempt for the common weal hardly implies a sympathy with the more delusional forms of nut-job populism that breed in small, strange pockets throughout the West. Nor, I suspect, would a full-blown Texas cage match between Martha Stewart and Karl Marx produce much good, though a few rounds in a back alley might not hurt.

Bald greed lamely attempts to conceal itself beneath righteous claims of private property in the moral equivalent of a comb-over. In the hallucinatory logic of the acquisitive, the Montana law permitting the public use of public waterways that flow through private land deprives the rightful owners of potential income from leasing their streamside property to fishing clubs and outfitters; they are denied the right to profit at public expense, a stipulation oddly missing from my copy of the Constitution. Expensive legal teams, assembled by these aggrieved victims, funded from the coffers of extractive industry, and aided by whatever elected finger puppets they are able to purchase, wave subpoenas and threaten "takings" litigation—an indigestibly rich irony considering who's doing all the taking. Consolidating their interests under cynically misleading rubrics like "Allies of the Land" and "Citizens for Responsible Use," they dress up their half-baked ideas to make them appear palatable and then serve them to the gullible, who can't see that even a honey-glazed, clove-studded, pineapple-garnished ham is still just a pig's ass, and only half a one at that.

That everything goes to the highest bidder is not an inevitable consequence of the flow of money into open space, just a frequent one. Nor are those bidders, individual or corporate, particularly numerous; that's the frightening part. Wealth makes itself felt far out of proportion to the number of the wealthy; that is in part what wealth means—the capacity to leave a footprint far larger than one's actual feet.

In twenty years, the middle space I inhabit has become a little less spacious and a little less in the middle, and the obvious irony does not escape me. I am here too, just like everyone else, complicit both as a temporary homesteader with a presence on the land and as a fisherman with one on the river. There is less of each to go around, and the landscape and the water are both hard used: diminishing roadless areas, fragmented wildlife corridors, fires, invasive species, competition for water, declining aquifers, altered runoff patterns, siltation, sewage and septic effluent, nutrient loading of waters. It's not a question of intentions. Most people believe themselves careful and responsible, and possibly most people are.

Light footprints are better than heavy ones, but even these can become too many. And they are headed only in the direction of too many more. Montana is landlocked, but the human sea level is rising here, as it is everywhere. We are becoming too numerous, and our unchecked enormity is a point often observed but less often pursued, since the corollaries, of problem and solution alike, make people profoundly uneasy.

Some summers back, a friend from Maine came out to stay at the ranch for a while. A kind of homesteader himself, he'd built his own house in the woods near the coast and arranged his life for about as much self-sufficiency as it is possible to realize in the modern world without declaring yourself a separate country—growing his own food, collecting his own water, self-employed, barely a blip on the grid. I showed him around the place and, as I'd anticipated, he took a keen interest in the old cabin, inspecting and commenting on its materials, design, and construction details, all of which were familiar to him from researching such matters before starting on his own place decades earlier. Leading him around to the rear of the cabin, I began explaining what little I'd gathered of its history and first occupants, walking on as I talked. I'd just about come to the end of what I knew when I realized that my friend was no longer behind me. He'd stopped not far from the back door and stooped over to examine a pair of small, shallow, sunken plots of earth, less than a dozen feet apart. The ground had been disturbed there long ago and had since weathered smooth and grown over in grass. He was deeply engrossed in these, and I wasn't sure he was even listening anymore. But I finished up the story anyway, telling him about the eleven children born here and adding what I had only recently been told, that all but a few had died in their youth, quite probably of cholera.

He straightened up and adjusted his cap. "I'm not surprised. That looks to have been the outhouse," he observed, pointing to one of the small depressions, "and that one," he said, pointing to the other, "the well."

7

THE MOST OF IT

One basic quality unites all the works of mankind that speak to us in human, recognizable voices across the barriers of time, culture, and space: the simple quality of being well made.

—Bill Reid

THE MOMENT BEFORE SHE CAUGHT FIRE, THE WOMAN IN THE WESTERN shirt asked me a question about fishing. I attached no special significance to this coincidence, particularly since it wasn't really a fire in the technical sense, more like what emergency professionals call a "smoke event," and certainly not a case of "bursting into flames," as the Painter would breathlessly describe it afterward. In any event, during the hours leading up to this incipient combustion, the Painter and I, along with a few other people, had been dining at the home of some casual acquaintances who lived near Ennis and had arranged a small get-together. Under ordinary circumstances, those of us at the ranch seldom socialize much beyond the confines of the house and cottonwoods, since we see one another infrequently enough as it is. But a couple of the dinner guests happened to be friends from the East whose company the Painter and I seldom get to enjoy, and so we'd accepted the invitation.

The evening's conversation revolved mostly around fishing and books, and the talk, as I recall, was lively, beginning as drinks were poured, proceeding without interruption through the meal, and continuing as we rose from the table some hours later and crowded our way to the small front hall in preparation for leaving. It was in these tight quarters that I found myself face to face with the woman in the western shirt, while she found herself back to back with a burning candle that sat on a small table behind her. But before either us noticed the tragic potential of her situation, she asked me, "What is your favorite place to fish?" At this point events took the unfavorable turn that I have described, though it proved a minor matter in the end, a little scorched cotton fabric, a few curls of smoke, a whiff of singed hair, more an awkwardness than a danger. The matter was dealt with quickly, caused no harm except to the western shirt, and absolutely did not require the rest of us to rush over and "put her out," as the Painter would report later at the ranch. In the small commotion that ensued, however, the matter of favorite water understandably fell by the wayside.

But her question stuck with me, in part because, like most fishermen, I have been asked it from time to time, though rarely with such emphasis, mostly by nonanglers in a well-intentioned gesture toward polite conversation. Despite its apparent simplicity, I am never sure quite how, or how much, to respond. I imagine that the woman in the western shirt anticipated that I would name the Madison, if only out of return politeness on my part, since she lived on its banks. And I probably would have done just that had our exchange not terminated in a "blazing inferno," as the Painter would insist in her subsequent account. It would not have been the most accurate of answers, but it would have been the mercifully short one. An honest reply would take some explaining, and I have learned that any response to a fishing question posed casually at a social function should be scrupulously brief, at least if you care to get invited anywhere again.

No doubt some anglers can give a ready answer, but I suspect that most of us would need to give it some serious thought and even then quite possibly fail to decide the issue satisfactorily. For the larger question immediately subdivides itself into a number of smaller, potentially relevant ones: the place, for instance, where you tend to catch the largest fish, or the most, or the most difficult or satisfying ones; or the place that fishes most consistently; or the one you automatically head to when you have some time; or that best conduces to the methods you prefer; and so on and so forth. Addressing even these second-order matters can present substantial difficulties, and because each might be answered differently, resolving them might not go far in settling the original question anyway.

Given its encumbrance with conditions and qualifications, many people might dismiss the question as invalid or meaningless to begin with. Moreover, the matter of a favorite place to fish has no practical importance whatsoever, and possibly none of any sort. Pursuing it further, they might argue, would be merely "academic," by which they mean pointlessly speculative, utterly immaterial, almost certainly unproductive. As one at least marginally affiliated with the academic world, I would take exception to this use of the word were it not so accurate in many instances. For it does convey the way we often operate, noodling around with ideas in the distant hope that something comes of it—funding, for instance. So perhaps we can look into favorite water in this same spirit of uncertainty, with the aim of just seeing if it leads anywhere. After all, most of us are called upon to address roughly analogous questions from time to time in our nonfishing lives. In choosing a spouse, for instance, the word "favorite" is not out of place and presents similar complexities. So I think the woman in the western shirt has posed a legitimate question, though in the case of favorite water, let us assume you may choose only once, just to keep the lawyers out of it and simplify things. The crucial preliminary, of course, comes in deciding exactly how you will construe the question. And determining what you mean by "favorite" in the first place is perhaps the most telling part of the whole inquiry since it reveals a good deal about you, which is another argument against trotting out the long answer in polite company.

Naturally, how you interpret the concept of "favorite" depends on how you look at things more generally, on that particular vantage point that exists at the intersection of the person you are and your circumstances in life at the moment. In my own case, that would be someone who, if the actuarial tables can be trusted and I am statistically representative, has just passed the midpoint of his serious fishing years, prior to which he dabbled around as a child with a fishing pole and after which he will almost certainly decline into childlike dabbling of many sorts. All in all, this is not a bad spot to be in; at a minimum, it offers a pretty good view in both directions. Presumably, much fishing lies ahead, but at the same time, the expression "the rest of your life" no longer represents the abstract infinity that it did in youth.

Discovering a useful meaning of "favorite" from among the numerous possibilities also depends upon how you go about looking for it in the first place, what people in my line of work like to call a "methodology." Mine involves not quite a triangulation, but more like a bracketing from fixed reference points that I learned in some physics courses I once took in college, where it was standard operating procedure. The method is perhaps best explained by an old joke often repeated by engineers, who purport to be a practical people, at the expense of physicists, who incline to the theoretical: If you ask a physicist to calculate the forces operating on a three-legged stool, he will first determine the forces on a hypothetical stool with no legs, then on an imaginary stool with an infinite number of legs;

having comfortably contained his solution between these outer limits, he will spend the rest of his life working out the problem of three legs. This approach has always appealed to me, in the abstract anyway. Its orderliness gives the impression, if largely illusory, that progress of some sort is being made, though in the end it frequently gets me no further than it does the average physicist, as you will probably see.

At any rate, in an attempt to gain some ground on the matter, I framed two different but closely related versions of the question about fishing places as a way of drawing a line of sorts around its farthest reaches, of bookending the extreme contexts of the word "favorite" in hopes of corralling some useful idea in the space between. First question: "If you had only one more day to fish for the rest of your life, where would you go?" And second: "If you had only one place to fish for the rest of your life, where would it be?" The distortions I've worked on the original question are obvious and inevitable, but I hope that the concept of "favorite" still visibly appears somewhere in the foreground and perhaps in a way that doesn't bias the term toward any interpretation in particular. Just how far my alternate versions will get us remains to be seen, but entertaining them might at least be a way to get started on a response to the woman in the western shirt. Both of my formulations, of course, represent fairly joyless prospects, though of different sorts, which stands to reason since they generally point in different directions. The first has a retrospective, summative, and quite possibly symbolic arc that might lead you, for instance, back to the place where you caught your first fish, or your first trout on a fly, or fished with someone important to you. The second version seems to me more speculative and forward-looking, practical and literal rather than symbolic, and involving a different sort of imagining. And given this divergence, an angler might well give a different answer to each.

At the same time, the two questions do overlap. Both, for instance, evoke a certain sense of finality and bring into play that vaguely obituary brand of reckoning that comes with contemplating an idea of the rest of your life, an exercise quite probably carried out in terms that do not pertain exclusively to fishing. This is one of the distortions introduced by my vantage point. More importantly, answering either one would almost certainly begin with taking stock of all the waters you've ever fished, canvassing your experience to see which place, if any, stands out so persuasively that you might choose to return there for the rest of your fishing life, however long or short that might be. To clarify the future through the lens of the past is sensible; we do it all the time. And a fortunate angler will be able to draw from a barrage of italicized memories of specific times spent in particular places.

Yet in the end, I suspect, this approach won't take us very far in answering either of the questions I proposed. In the first place, such recollections assume a highlight-film quality; they are apt to be fragments of the extraordinary or idiosyncratic —that is why we remember them. Second, all of these glimpses of separate days on disparate waters are, in all likelihood, memorable for different reasons. Some, for instance, probably involved fish; some didn't; some could have, but if they did that's not what you recall about them. What you do remember remains more or less singular to each recollection. In a general way, they all represent good times in good places, but in the matter of getting you closer to the meaning of "favorite," they lead you in different directions simultaneously. From an aerial view, they present an indistinct and inconclusive pattern. And perhaps more to the point, while you may return to the waters of the past, the past itself is irretrievable; that kind of going back is not possible. I believe several southerners have written whole books to this effect.

So searching to interpret "favorite" through a history that might repeat itself, in a sense by generalizing from the specific, may not finally clarify much or bring us any closer to a comfortable stipend. Possibly, the opposite direction holds more promise—using the abstract to converge on the concrete, sifting out the similarities among all of these recollections, looking for what they share, some kind of root-level denominators common to them all. Collectively, I suppose, you might call these something like "what you value" in fishing. Or you might call them something else, but a place that has them in abundance would appear to qualify as a favorite. And here, what you have probably sensed hovering in the background now makes itself explicit: that any conception about a favorite place to fish cannot be separated from an idea of why you fish to begin with, of what you go to the water looking for and what, having been there, you come away with. Answering any of the questions, then, about fishing places moves beyond defining "favorite" to determining, in a sense, what you mean by "fishing."

Unfortunately, this does not simplify things much, since the second term is no less slippery than the first and changes over time. Younger anglers, for instance, generally hold a kinetic and omnivorous view of angling, fishing intensely, physically, and somewhat indiscriminately, always hungry except when they are full. Older fishermen, on the other hand, form attachments. The parameters surrounding when and where and why they fish become narrower. They would like to think it a case of greater discrimination, but this confuses refinement with personal preference, and more rarefied tastes with the general decelerations of mortality. Anglers of a certain age and experience merely get a little persnickety about fishing, just like trout of a certain age and experience. It isn't a matter of sophistication; in both cases, they've developed certain peculiarities that have helped them survive.

Either way, however, young or old, we have our standards, complex and mutable as they might be, that speak to the reasons we fish and what we value in it, and these would seem material to answering the question about a favorite place. And so perhaps by weaving a set of criteria, filtering through them all the waters of our experience, and seeing what's left behind, we may get somewhere. We reason in this fashion routinely. Some people even choose mates this way, relying on algorithms employed by a thriving industry of computerized "compatibility services." I'm told it sometimes works, and perhaps we'll get lucky tonight.

A partial list of my own criteria for such a place, to take one example, would include a medium-sized river with clear water in the shallows shading to a jade translucence in the deeper spots; a cobbled bottom that's pleasurable to wade; lots of thigh-deep riffles just choppy enough to hide minor mistakes; but also pools and slots and cutbanks that hide their mysteries; fishing that is neither uninterestingly easy nor impossibly demanding and always intriguingly varied; an abundance of aquatic insects, preferably in the larger sizes, that hatch on a civilized schedule; and generously proportioned trout that rise well to dry flies. The water must also possess certain less easily expressed attributes: a sense of promise, an atmosphere of quiet refuge, and a capacity for surprise; it must bespeak hope, engage the imagination, delight the soul, fulfill the need for an unmediated experience of the natural world, and reward the spirit in ways that go beyond fish even as it offers plenty of trout to get you started. All in all, pretty standard stuff. But when you get right down to actually filtering the waters of your experience, the problem with the conditions I've described, or any others that you could name, is that many rivers fulfill some of them but not others, and some rivers meet all of them but only at highly localized times and places. Depending on how rigid and numerous your criteria, they end up capturing most of the places you fish or none at all. So in one respect, they don't take you very far in answering the question about a favorite place, which perhaps we might define here as the water that best approximates the conditions of our greatest satisfaction.

But in another respect, we may have made some headway by suggesting that a favorite place may be envisioned less as a specific geographical spot than as a set of circumstances. That is, a fishing place (and fishing itself, I would argue) is a kind of shorthand—a metonym, like "Montana" or "the ranch," that names the container for the things contained. Some of those things, the state of the fish and water and weather, for example, lie beyond your control, the eternal mutabilities of location. Others, however, represent consequences of your own choosing. The particular ways in which you appreciate a river, for instance; the assumptions and intentions you bring to it; the way you envision what you are doing on the water and what you take its purpose to be; what you attend to and the person you become while you are there—all of these, and others, are contained in a space called "favorite" that we partly define for ourselves by what we choose to invest in it. I doubt that these choices even register on us consciously. In our minds, it's just how we fish, invisibly there, like a form of gravity.

To say that a favorite water may be less a place than a state of affairs may be to do no more than advance the unremarkable observation that, in considering the question, we imagine for ourselves a kind of ideal place. Tom McGuane once observed that when you inventory the rivers of your life and distill their essentials from memory, they come more and more to resemble one another, until finally "the trout fisherman finishes his life with but one river," a kind of "Platonic gem." And perhaps in answering the question of a favorite place, this is the water we are somehow trying to name. That such places exist only in the imagination doesn't stop us from fishing; we will go wherever and whenever we can. For most of us, the opportunity is scarce enough even on lesser waters, and as I was warned repeatedly in various contexts while growing up, "You just have to make the most of it." I wouldn't recognize for quite some time that this did not necessarily counsel resignation in the face of a diminished reality but could be taken as an injunction to create, to fashion a well-made thing in whatever small ways are available.

In the end, the particulars of whatever ideal we might construct are less significant than the fact that many of those specifics do not originate with the fish or the fishing or the place itself; they are a product of the fisherman. To some extent, and possibly a large one, we create the places we fish through the decisions we make about what matters there. A river, or a lake, or a saltwater flat is fundamentally itself. But it also contains the raw material from which to arrange a place of meaningful occupation, one that grants a temporary autonomy, where the miraculous in the ordinary is more likely to show itself and where you are more likely to see it, where you can inhabit a story you fashion that is all about why you are there. The great majority of anglers lead lives of small liberations, and this sense of an independent space arranged to accommodate the shape of our best imaginings is perhaps familiar in some form to most of us, as I think it is to anyone who answers to any place that urges itself on the soul.

We have, as I feared, come no great distance and perhaps none at all in answering the question posed by the woman in the western shirt, and I suppose that at this point even a token honorarium is out of the question. Besides, my own favorite water, could I even decide on it, would be of interest to no one. But in its roundabout way, this may be as close as I can come to explaining, in a theoretical sense, how we arrive at the places we invent.

8

Patterns of Behavior

If the facts don't fit the theory, change the facts.

—Albert Einstein

Despite strong evidence to the contrary, I still suspect that the average trout fisherman possesses more intelligence than the average trout. This is not a lofty benchmark for either, nor are the discrepancies always perceptible. And you will find exceptions; like most of angling's larger propositions, this one holds true except when it doesn't. Here the matter of fly patterns leaps to mind with disturbing readiness. When it comes to flies, the fish have the advantage. At the end of the day, only the trout's opinion counts, though this does not stop anglers from having plenty of their own. If anything, it eggs them on.

Fishermen do not necessarily behave like rational creatures, but we are, after our own fashion, creatures of reason, driven or inclined to explanatory conjectures. Simply catching fish or failing to catch them does not serve; the unrepeatable successes and persistent failures haunt us equally. We must know the causes, and if they cannot be objectively discovered, we will invent them. We generally prefer to anyway since it's easier. Part of this tendency originates in fly fishing itself. I cannot call to mind another sport that so openly invites the more analytical forms of observation, so insistently encourages the construction of hypotheses, and so seldom rewards them. The quality of a day's fishing, whether good, bad, or otherwise, can rarely be attributed to a single factor; almost always it involves a conspiracy. Fly angling is an occupation of a thousand variables—water and weather, light and temperature, instincts and accidents—in which a small alteration in any one of them may rattle down to the others in a chain reaction and cascade through the system until everything, most particularly the fishing, changes. Or not, depending. You might, like a well-adjusted person, accept the fundamental inscrutability of this mechanism and be satisfied with what comes your way. Or you can, like a fisherman, try to figure it out, erecting little systems of understanding about where and when to fish and what to use; we like to call this "problem solving," though the term describes the intention more accurately than the results.

But the effort itself constitutes one of our defining characteristics; we are famous theorists. Many of us are better at it than we are at actual fishing. Put a nickel into a fly angler and he will dispense theories until you put a quarter in to make him stop or, failing that, manually unplug him. Set him loose on a trout stream and he may not bring home dinner, but he will return with enough miraculous hypotheses about fish and fishing to feed multitudes of the credulous. Because failure occasions most of these explanations, they tend to the exculpatory, but we do not advance them to rationalize or dismiss the past; they represent conceptual architectures with which to build the fishing of a better future. "Next time," we say.

The ordinary challenges of abstract reasoning are much reduced for the angler, since he does not regard a deficiency of facts as any great obstacle and willingly manufactures vast generalities from a single, sometimes clearly anomalous fishing event. That a trout should come to his fly, for instance, at the moment a commercial airliner passes overhead provides sufficient foundation for an intricate edifice of speculation involving Bernoulli's principle, fluctuations in the barometric column, visual parallax, disruptive acoustic vibrations transmitted to the streambed, anticipatory feeding by the trout, and so forth. This does not so much suggest impaired faculties as enthusiasm, and if such theoretical constructs have much in common with a one-legged stool, the angler will happily point out that they might still bear weight if you sit just so. I have seen peddled in print tortured accounts that explain why the fishing is always better under power lines that cross a river and why trout bite best on Thursdays. Naturally, as a fisherman I have done my share of this kind of thinking, but then I was trained as an academic and ruined by design. And, too, beyond a few obvious and largely unhelpful überfacts—that the fishing, for instance, will sometimes be good and sometimes not—fly angling offers little in the way of absolutes; for the most part, it consists mainly of conjectures forcibly willed to the status of fact. Frequently these are published for general consumption, where they always call to mind a full-sized *Tyrannosaurus rex* skeleton I saw as a child and greatly admired until I learned it had been entirely reconstructed from two or three vertebrae, a knuckle bone, and a broken tooth. The rest was just plaster of Paris and surmise.

The serious angler builds his most elaborate conjectures around trout flies, the few that have succeeded, the many that have failed, and those that surely would have worked had he only thought to bring them. Fly patterns assume a high importance on the Madison in part for the same reason they do almost everywhere: not because the fly plays such a decisive role in our fishing but because it represents one of the few knowns in a system composed largely of unknowns. We regard it as the one component of angling most directly under our control—in terms of selection, if not necessarily presentation. We operate under the theory that a change of fly offers the surest route to a change in fortune. For an overwhelming number of us, of course, the best way to catch more fish is to become a better fisherman. This is a wearying thought, however, and perhaps best postponed for the time being, though absolutely our number one priority for next season, when we can start fresh and apply our fullest concentration. I, for one, can hardly wait, but right now I believe I'll just give this chartreuse Humpy a try instead. This isn't solely a matter of taking the easy way, although we do conveniently forget the fact that knotting on a different fly requires infinitely less time and personal effort than learning how to do something new or better. Rather, to a significant extent we approach fishing itself through the patterns we use. The fly, we reason, is what makes things happen, and so using a different one should make them happen differently.

I believe that this thinking is flawed, but not totally flawed. Returning to the same water year after year does sacrifice some variety and range in one's fishing; on a river like the Madison, however, it does prove instructive in the matter of trout flies. You get a long-term view of the way in which they go in and out of style; like haute cuisine and haircuts, fly patterns enjoy temporary vogues, chic for a season and forgotten the next, if they last even that long. In part, the familiar engines of marketing fuel this turnover as they propel the tiny wheels of a fly shop, which these days is quite likely careening helplessly toward Chapter 11. A changing inventory delivers what the American customer has been trained to seek most—the new and improved, though in a pinch he will settle for updated packaging. To return to a fly shop time after time and find only the same dusty Sofa Pillows and wilted Pheasant Tails would disappoint us, purely as consumers, as surely as visiting an automobile showroom and discovering that this year's models, regrettably, show no change in the number of cup holders.

But novelty for profit does not entirely explain the fluctuating trends in flies. Part of it occasionally makes sense. On the Madison, and a few other western rivers I've fished, certain patterns sometimes ascend to an immense, if brief, popularity for the highly defensible reason that they actually catch more fish—a phenomenon that most anglers think of as the "hot fly" effect. It has nothing to do with hatches. Certainly hatches can have their hot flies, but this never surprises us. That one PMD pattern consistently raises more trout than another, even very similar one seems perfectly natural to us even if we cannot pinpoint exactly why the first works better than the second, though of course we are never without our speculations. The hot flies I refer to fall into that loose category of attractor patterns—typically overscaled, overdressed, and if not brazenly gaudy, at least tarted up a good bit. In some unspecified way, this accounts to us for their "attraction."

We fish attractor dry flies on the Madison quite regularly, in part because the river invites them—wide, shallow, clear, and so stony that nearly every square yard of water looks worth a cast or two—and in part because prospecting with big dry flies persuades you to a casual and relaxed rhythm. Blind fishing has as its most immediate objective a good cast, which after a time becomes its own incentive; you grow more absorbed in throwing strikes and less concerned about getting them. It is far less emotionally strenuous than, say, contending with the sense of disempowerment and personal insufficiency that sometimes attends a hatch. Though the purist derides the nymph angler for his yarn and foam indicators, I think that searching the water with a big attractor pattern comes much closer to bobber fishing in a psychological sense; they engage the visual imagination in similar ways. It would be inaccurate to call attractor fishing a lazy man's occupation, but it can rather easily incline toward indolence and sometimes tumble over into the pleasantly mindless. In the Montana I've invented, this isn't an unacceptable way to fish.

One of the first summers we stayed at the ranch, we discovered, as had nearly everyone else on the river, that a Royal Wulff was the hot fly. This pattern has a long and noble history on Montana rivers; a bit old-fashioned, it is nonetheless staunch and of distinguished lineage, not always the star but a good team player, and still standard issue for most western anglers. While more fashionable patterns have eclipsed it over time, the Royal Wulff continues to be a credible opening gambit and a solid fallback fly. But during that summer almost twenty years ago, it turned hot as a plasma torch. It didn't roll every trout in the river, but the fly worked about as effectively as a searching pattern can. The following year, though we fished the Royal Wulff with a zeal that gradually declined into grim obstinacy, its stock had dropped to eight cents on the dollar. Instead, the Trude was paying big dividends; we caught fish on little else. The summer after that, nothing produced especially well. The Mechanic makes it his business to sniff out these new prospects and keep us current, and through the years we've watched other hot attractors come and go, some whose success ended as abruptly as it began, others that ramped up gradually, hit peak temperatures for a few weeks or a season, then cooled off and became just ordinary flies again.

Attractor patterns, especially the hot ones but also as a general category, are the subject of much speculation among anglers and of particular note because they require reversing the customary direction of our theorizing. Normally, we head to the river, and from all the information we can observe—water clarity, level, and temperature; wind, sun, and weather; bugs or no bugs; recent rain or drought; time of the season; hour of the day; phase of the moon—along with whatever our own angling histories make available to us, we attempt to deduce a plausible answer to the question, "What fly should, or could, work?" With attractor patterns, you catch the fish first and ask afterward, "Why on earth would a trout eat this?" Among the most orthodox anglers, all theories spring from a single assumption—that a trout fly mimics some form of trout food—and its corollary—that the nature of the imitation can be established through a sufficiently rigorous inquiry. An attractor pattern, as a rule, looks less like a bug than the idea of a bug as reproduced by a person who's never actually seen one and has relied on descriptions given by someone with a pathological fear of insects—like a police artist's sketch of a suspect rendered from the account of a hysterical victim. This questionable relation of art to life complicates the matter of identification but does not deter the dogmatist, and it is dumbfounding at times to watch him apply the rack and thumbscrews of his presuppositions to a fly like the Royal Wulff or Trude, trying to extract the secret of what it simulates. Some of the technical fishing books contain transcripts of these interrogations, appalling in their brutality and contradictory in results. A spruce moth one minute, a flying ant the next, a Trude will tell you whatever it thinks you want to hear because it doesn't know anything. It swears there's nothing to confess, that this is all some terrible mistake.

I, for one, believe it's telling the truth. But in doing so, I merely replace one set of assumptions with another: my own, formulated decades ago when I first began using attractor patterns on the brook-trout streams of the Blue Ridge Mountains. At about the same time, and quite by chance, I happened to reread one of Edgar Allan Poe's famous tales of ratiocination, "The Purloined Letter." In one part of this story, the Paris police search the home of an unscrupulous government minister, trying to recover a stolen letter containing sensitive information with which he is blackmailing the queen. The police know the minister to be a devious and clever man and conduct a meticulous investigation—even probing the chair cushions with long needles and examining the furniture joints with a microscope to detect evidence of a secret compartment in which the document might be concealed. They leave having found nothing, and we learn that the thief has simply placed the letter in a cheap wooden card rack hanging on the wall—hidden in plain sight. One runs across this idea from time to time in real life—the fugitive who eludes a manhunt, for instance, by sitting in the lobby of the courthouse drinking tea and reading the newspaper. I think about attractor patterns in these same terms, though I have found the idea most usefully formulated in a play written by William Congreve some two hundred years before the Royal Wulff was even invented:

No mask, like open truth, to cover lies;

As to go naked is the best disguise.

Trout, I suspect, look at an attractor pattern and refuse to acknowledge the truth of what they see. Something so outrageously unfoodlike in appearance, they seem to believe, must be edible; why else would it go to such lengths to look like it isn't? Attractors employ a reverse psychology of some sort—I haven't fully worked out this part of the theory yet—in which the fish are blinded by obviousness. Because anglers often resemble trout in just this way, the whole idea has the kind of tidy symmetry I appreciate in a theory.

The phenomenon of the hot pattern illuminates another part of the angling psyche by furnishing the most conspicuous instance of a generality that all fishermen accept: some flies simply produce better results than others. This recognition gives rise to a not wholly fraudulent line of thinking: the comparative (one fly works better than another) implies the superlative (one of them must work best). And as new fly patterns continue to appear, it stands to reason that the best keeps getting better. From a theoretical standpoint, however, this advance finally has an upper limit, and somewhere in the future, perhaps not far away, the best fly that could ever be awaits discovery. It doesn't matter if you envision this fly as a general-purpose pattern, a fly for all seasons, or one aimed at a specific circumstance—the green drake hatch, for example; it is the same idea on a different scale. This hypothetical pattern often presents itself to the imagination as the "perfect fly," though we willingly concede that such a thing could never exist in the literal sense. At least we don't think so. But then again we are the same people who, as eight-year-olds in a furtive and quivering hopefulness, ordered X-Ray Specs from the back of a comic book, even as we knew that they could not possibly work because . . . well, if they did, you'd see a lot more of them around.

Fly fishermen do not universally share this belief in the perfect fly, but it's probably held by nearly all anglers who tie their own flies and by a great many who do not. For even spectacular fishing carries with it a nagging sense that your fly is ringing up sales with only a small fraction of the available customers. Should you, for example, drift a five-mile stretch of the Madison, you would probably float past ten- or fifteen-thousand trout; from a rough statistical standpoint—and on a banner day, let's say—it does not seem like a modest one thousand strikes would be too much to ask. Realistically speaking, of course, on the trip of a lifetime, if you are both lucky and good, you might get one hundred. The as-yet-unrealized pattern, we can all agree, would not raise fifteen thousand trout in a day, but it would, we are pretty sure, be a lot, lot better than what we use now.

The notion of this fly, in the abstract alone, points to a version of fishing that presupposes a kind of Ultimate Truth, which, its seekers understand, almost certainly cannot be attained and quite possibly does not even exist. I suppose this sort of ambiguity has always surrounded ultimate truths in general, but historically speaking, it does not appear ever to have stopped anyone from looking for them. All trout flies are imperfect, but some are less imperfect than others, and how much less becomes the question. Any trout fly that catches a trout gives some fragmentary hint of the ideal, a partial glimpse into a transcendent reality that we will probably never arrive at. New patterns keep coming, however, to reenergize the faith and propel us forward, and once you board that train, there's no telling where you'll end up. "Relics of the true cross abound," Robert Hunter once observed, "sufficient to crucify a small army of saviors." In the end, this search for salvation may be what prevents us from becoming better fishermen.

The failure, so far, to obtain the perfect fly leaves us only with our deficient approximations and the assorted rationales for them that we bring to the water. They fill our fly boxes, which themselves then constitute a kind of metatheory, gathering together, without necessarily reconciling, all the discrete and sometimes self-contradictory conjectures about trout that we have embodied in trout flies and accumulated over the years in our vests. Our flies may not be organized, but they do possess a kind of logic—just not the same logic for everyone. Consult the fly boxes of a dozen different anglers on a single river like the Madison, and you may find it difficult to see how all these people are in the same business. One selection reveals the rationale of historical or sentimental attachment: Catskill patterns, traditional designs, classics—the navy blazer and gray flannels of fly fishing. Another angler favors patterns that correspond scrupulously to the life cycles of aquatic insects that he's been told will hatch at certain places and times but almost never do—the more fashionable contemporary logic of science. One person carries no nymphs; another carries nothing but. The relative proportions of attractor patterns like the Renegade, general-purpose patterns like the Hare's Ear, and special-purpose flies like the Quigley Cripple exhibit telling variations. You might discover a penchant for parachute patterns or hackleless styles; a fondness for highly realistic flies or suggestively impressionistic ones; a preference for patterns burdened with so much lead or tungsten that they do not seem so much tied as mined. Everyone has his own idea about the thing. Yet the trout are always themselves; they do not behave differently for different people, though I admit they do seem more congenial to the better anglers. Still, we all confront the same observed evidence on the water, reach into our fly boxes, and, often enough, produce different solutions to the problem of catching fish.

What our flies have in common, though, is that all of them signify something we believe in, or used to believe in, or think we might believe in when we get around to trying them. Dig through an angler's patterns and you will unearth a private archaeology of shrewd inferences and failed speculations, unlikely hopes, long-shot bets, the remnants of rivers past, hatches that materialized or didn't but still might. And if that angler ties his own flies, you will also find a hundred experiments gone monstrously wrong for every one that worked even a little. Our fly boxes warehouse our experience and experiences; they become a form of material memory not total recall, of course, just scattered bits and pieces, like regular memory. They record our ongoing surmises about how trout see and recognize a fly, the principles by which they interpret it, and the ways they may react. On the one hand, the reasoning behind our fly patterns amounts to a kind of mythmaking that explains why things are the way they are; on the other, our explanations are like performance art and all quite mystifying. Either way, they bear the stamp of our individual minds. Our theories are impressed with something of who we are, and the choice of patterns we carry discloses something about us. Like pets, fly boxes take on the personalities of their owners; they house our angling identities, which may or may not resemble our everyday identities as they exist uncorrupted by fishing. It depends upon the fisherman.

* * *

The Painter chooses flies with a cautious restraint, remaining loyal to those that have served her well in the past, and so her fly boxes reiterate the most widespread form of question begging in a sport already notorious for circularities of logic: I mostly fish these patterns because I catch most of my fish on them. This conservatism in the matter of flies is atypical for the Painter, who, in real life, is an unconventional and creative thinker. But it is not entirely unprecedented, either. She will not, for instance, eat anything cooked that looks like it did when it was alive, an idiosyncrasy that makes the refrigerator in our kitchen strongly resemble her fly boxes as a repository of the solidly familiar. When presented with a new fly pattern, she reacts as skeptically as most trout, rising guardedly for an inspection, then turning away in refusal. I can sometimes induce her to try a fly she's never used before, but it must deliver the goods in short order as she sees no reason to flog an underachiever when a proven performer might just as easily be put to work.

Getting results with a fly, while a necessary condition, does not in itself completely suffice, and she tempers her otherwise committed empiricism by what I suppose comes down to a painterly eye. A new pattern must meet her aesthetic standards, which have nothing to do with a pattern looking "pretty," to her the superficial and irrelevant appraisal of a nonangler. Nor do they require that a fly look "buggy" or "fishy," in the way ordinary anglers understand these ideas. Though she has tried to articulate her criteria to me, such things do not lend themselves easily to words, and as nearly as I can figure, a fly must appear sufficiently "dignified" and in some unspecifiable way exhibit a sense of self-respect. Since the Painter teaches Romantic and Victorian literature, I suppose this conflation of the artistic and the moral should not come as a surprise. Whatever the measure, she knows it when she sees it and will dismiss those patterns that in her own reckoning appear vulgar, tawdry, cheap, grotesque, or, I guess, lacking in ethical fiber. On the other hand, any fly that catches fish automatically goes a long way to becoming beautiful in her estimation, which if nothing else underscores the complicated and elastic nature of aesthetic categories.

In still a more fundamental visual sense, she insists that a pattern be detectable by the naked eye—not smaller than, say, size 18 or so. If she cannot see it, she will not use it, no matter how well it works, which means, in the first place, that she fishes only dry flies. I have occasionally persuaded her to try one of the less self-endangering forms of nymph fishing—a high-floating dry fly with a beadhead dropper—but despite some impressive successes, she regards the thing as cheesy and redundant—"Like wearing a belt and suspenders at the same time," as she once described it. In her interpretation of fly fishing, a trout that refuses a dry fly is a trout hardly worth catching as it, too, lacks self-respect, and she will continue fishing until she finds one that can behave properly. Her theories about fly patterns are grounded primarily in the relevance of history, aesthetic gratification, and the efficacy of pure determination.

The Cook and the Bodhi generally approach the flies they use with a kind of passive omnivorousness. Perhaps because they do a bit of tying, if only infrequently and never on a self-sustaining basis, they entertain all trout flies with a more open mind; that having been said, when it comes to new patterns their fly boxes do not exactly brim with initiative. Of the two, the Cook shows somewhat more enterprise in this respect. Though he has fly-fished for half his life, he is the youngest among us and the most romantic by temperament; the kind of ambitious hopefulness surrounding new things that often typifies one's earlier angling years will surface in flashes, and from time to time he'll arrive at the ranch with some fresh prospects in his fly boxes. He doesn't make a habit of it, however, and for the most part neither he nor the Bodhi experiment much on their own with unfamiliar flies. But should someone offer, they will accept a new pattern and fish it willingly, even if the theory of its design strikes them as improbable or, as has happened on occasion, completely preposterous. They have been around enough to know that, where fish are concerned, almost anything is possible. They will remind you that the supernaturally selective creature snubbing the angler's best moves during a midge hatch and the chamber of commerce trout hogging down Cheetos thrown from a bridge by tourists are in fact the same animal. They also understand the implications of this, which do not offer a terribly productive starting point for translating theories about trout into actual trout flies.

At the same time, their view of trout fosters a certain absence of prejudice in the matter, and in the interests of scientific inquiry and possibly better fishing, they'll happily test-drive any fly I give them, with a startlingly high, though not infinite, tolerance for failure. After a futile hour or two, you may see their resolve begin to blister and peel and sometimes slough off in great patches. But even then, sufficient cheerleading can keep them at it for much of the day. In this regard, they react very unlike the Painter, who expects a potentially better pattern to be actually better rather quickly and so sometimes leaps to premature condemnations. But she also forgives more easily over the long term and can be convinced to fish the same loser on two or three different occasions, provided they are widely spaced. A pattern that disappoints the Cook or the Bodhi after a liberal trial period gets rejected as a failed concept for all eternity.

The Cook always arrives at the water well supplied with flies, and in one respect, his fly boxes resemble my own in that he carries multiple backups, as many as a dozen sometimes, of selected patterns and sizes—a #12 Stimulator, for instance. If my own motives are any indication, the redundancy suggests equal parts optimism and anxiety, the hope that someday one of those flies will turn hot and the corresponding worry that when it does you might not have enough of them. He carries a good many fly boxes on the water, and while they do not signify a confidence that the mysteries of trout will be unlocked by a fly pattern, they do represent some hope for a little clarification in the matter.

The Bodhi's fly boxes, much like the Bodhi, are consummately practical in their way—somewhat varied in their contents but also pared down to only one or two of each pattern, with a few exceptions. Like any pragmatist's, his selection of flies tilts heavily toward nymphs, though like everyone, he prefers to fish the dry fly. But he also believes in taking the shortest distance between two points, one of those points being near the bottom of the river where most of the trout live. His range of pattern types would appear to suggest that he thinks variety is at least moderately useful; in fact, almost nothing about flies matters much to him except having one tied on. Patterns have just accumulated in his boxes over the years, and while he has his favorites, he pretty much subscribes to the theory that if you put a fly—almost any fly—in front of a willing trout, it will bite. Much in fly fishing substantiates this, despite contemporary trends toward overcomplication. While the Bodhi by no means opposes a fly that would catch more trout, he will expend no great effort trying to find it.

The Mechanic, by nature, is intrigued by all innovation in the useful arts and enthusiastically embraces new fly patterns, most especially the hot and the haute, with which he comes well equipped each summer. Typically, these are nymphs, and he will fish them religiously until he loses the last one. And typically, they are underperformers that he doesn't replace. What remains in his vest afterward consists of a large supply of Woolly Buggers, mostly in black, and a few kilos of split shot. He takes many trout with these every year, including his fair share from the large-and-tall-men's department.

When it comes to the ways in which fly fishermen perceive their flies, one of the most meaningful dividing lines separates those who tie them from those who don't. I believe that anglers who tie simply think about their flies differently than do sensible and thrifty people who buy them. The preference for types and designs, the gravitation toward certain materials, even the tying techniques we employ all represent choices, and we choose in accordance with who we are. We invest something of ourselves in the making of our flies, and so they speak to our angling identities in more varied and complex ways. This certainly holds true of the flies that the Photographer ties. He spent several years guiding full-time, and many of the patterns he carries still embody the virtues one comes to appreciate when sitting down every night to tie flies for the next day's clients: they are quick to dress, durable, and expendable. They also catch fish, though to watch the Photographer on the water is in fact to be schooled in the presentationist philosophy of fly fishing, which elevates technique over technology and believes more in the skill of the delivery than in the contents of the package. Both his tying and his fishing suggest, if not an indifference to fly patterns, at least a certain workmanlike outlook on them.

Yet his fly boxes tell a different story. I have never met a fisherman more exacting about his flies. To begin with, he carries an unimaginable number of them, possibly a vestige of his guiding days, and comes prepared every season with an extensive supply of new ideas to try, sometimes patterns he has reproduced or modified from examples, more often designs of his own that he's fiddling around with in the way fly tiers do. He experiments incessantly, and his boxes frequently contain half a dozen versions of a specific idea in progress, each differing in some small particular that alters its look or behavior in the water or makes it simpler to tie. Most of these patterns, still climbing the evolutionary ladder, have no names; ask him what he's using and you'll get a recipe. He owns few standard patterns and seldom uses them. In fact, only under unusual circumstances can he be induced to use any fly he has not tied himself. And even then, regardless of how effective it might prove, he is apt to fish it politely for a short time, clip it from his leader, and substitute one of his own. It has nothing to do with arrogance or competitiveness; he does not necessarily believe that his own flies work better, only that they are more interesting to him.

This fussiness expresses itself in other ways, and in some of them the angler he most closely resembles is, oddly, the Painter. His photo work, for instance, frequently brings him into contact with fly tiers, from well-known names to ordinary amateurs, and he is the only angler I have ever known who refuses to fish flies that were designed by, named after, or otherwise representative of someone he dislikes. This is, to be sure, an extremely small number of people—the Photographer gets along with almost everyone. But his flies, like the Painter's, appear to involve rigorous moral distinctions, which I find peculiar in a man who seldom judges harshly in real life. Moreover, he shares the Painter's sense of fly aesthetics—not her particular standards, just the fact of having some. An unappealing fly gets dismissed as "interesting," his adjective of choice for human folly in all its forms and, as it pertains to flies, a euphemism for a pattern that would never be allowed to pollute his leader. A fly such as the Chernobyl Ant, for instance, inflicts an especial torture on him, and he grows visibly depressed just looking at one. A pattern that measures up, on the other hand, gets the only form of approval that matters to him: "I'd fish it."

A committed hatch fisherman, the Photographer coordinates his angling year to hit the right waters at the right times, chasing trout by chasing bugs, and all summer long he roams the northern Rockies, moving from river to river as their insects come into season and their fish to the surface. The only trout that exist to him are the ones that rise, the rest are forgettable and irrelevant. He recognizes this for the decadence that it is, but an angler with means, motive, and opportunity will always indulge his private extravagances. His fly boxes primarily hold dry flies and emerger patterns, along with a few small and light nymphs for shallow fishing. I believe that coaching countless clients in the more industrial forms of nymphing has left him with no appetite for it now. When he quit guiding, he blowtorched his remaining supply of split shot into a small lead disc and hurled it into the Pacific Ocean—figuratively speaking, anyway. He refuses to carry attractor patterns, under the theory that a fly that looks like an actual bug should be attraction enough. Frequently this is the case.

Like the Photographer and a great many other anglers, I also tie my own flies, and people who tie as I do—slowly—end up spending a fair amount of time with each one. You get to know them—not as individuals, of course, except for the occasional freaks that appear in your vise; those you remember. Rather, you grow familiar with the particular styles you favor. And just as a fly box comes to express the personality of its owner, so too certain patterns acquire personalities of their own based on how easy or difficult they are to tie, how well or badly you do it, how much or little you enjoy their materials, and what the trout say about them in the end. Close relationships develop. While a fly pattern obviously has no inner life, it does have the suggestion of one: a name, a parentage, a history, an occupation; it can evoke affection, trust, misgiving, prejudice; it has a finite lifespan and, as with people, its passing is sometimes mourned and sometimes not. A fly pattern is not a person, but collectively in our boxes flies do constitute a kind of population. Because we have made them and sometimes invented them and so know them in a way that the nontier does not, we don't so much use our flies as enter into partnerships with them.

I carry a number of patterns—the Copper John is a good example—with which I have uneasy relationships. The capriciousness of their hot-and-cold performance borders on willful behavior and has at times been the occasion for harsh words. I have said some things I've later regretted. Nevertheless, we've managed to stay together over the years, having learned to accept each other's shortcomings and capacities for disappointment. Other patterns in my boxes, mainly those of my own design, are destined to join the swelling ranks of those already forcibly ejected from my vest. For various reasons, things just didn't work out. Some boded ill from the beginning and went downhill from there; others, to all appearances packed with potential, threw away a promising future. Though I invested time in their upbringing, they now just loaf around and take up space. Some flies, particularly hatch-specific imitations, are strictly business associates. The Rusty Spinner, for instance, a fine fly within its area of expertise, is ultimately a specialist, and I have never warmed to it. We both just do our jobs and go home. I carry some patterns I never use, like the Black-Nosed Dace, solely because I think I ought to, having once come to believe that no well-stocked fly box should be without one. There are a few, like the Muddler Minnow and the standard Adams, that I just like having around. I sometimes use them, generally with unexceptional results, and have come to regard them like the well-intentioned old acquaintances you might call for a hand in fixing the roof or moving the furniture. They may not be of much help in the end, but you can always count on them to show up.

My fly boxes contain their share of new patterns and novel designs, and I spend some time every season experimenting with them, even those of suspect provenance or dubious prospects. While I like to think of myself as an equal-opportunity angler, I have limits and draw the line at those increasingly popular patterns, mostly nymphs and streamers, draped in more flashy glitter and trashy bling than a pop-star entourage, and dressed with a similar unholy sense of color. People will sometimes press one of these eyesores upon me, along with accounts of its devastating effectiveness. And I don't doubt them. That's exactly the problem: knowing that trout will eat such a fly lowers them in my estimation. To be honest, it sort of ruins things for me. I don't think trout should behave this way, which in itself goes some distance toward explaining my own fly boxes. For some reason, I believe that the fish and I ought to be operating under the same rough set of rules and following a story line at least loosely based on the workings of the natural world and its various moving parts. This assumption certainly leaves ample room for mystery and surprise but most certainly does not include fish with an appetite for tiny Las Vegas showgirls strapped to a hook shank. Conventional attractor patterns are about as far as I'm willing to stretch the matter, and only then because I am more forgiving of dry flies than of any other type.

This is merely my opinion, but it is also a fact of sorts. The trout in my universe have never been interested in sequin-and-paste costume simply because I have never shown it to them. In making this choice, and many others, I manage to supervise reality in a way that makes it conform to my worldview, which I take to be the ultimate theory behind all flies and fishing.

I suspect that fishermen have always held strong and sometimes complicated opinions about their flies. The evidence lies everywhere in the old books—the enthusiasms about "killing patterns," notions about how specific imitations should be fished during certain seasons, the minute and doting particulars about materials. It all sounds quite familiar to the modern angler, possibly because artificial flies have changed relatively little over the centuries. Styles, of course, come and go; that is the nature of style. But even many of the earliest patterns would not look noticeably out of place in a modern fly box. And while new ideas have come about and old ones been updated, the essential architecture of trout flies, their informing ideas, and a great many of the materials have remained fairly consistent. I have no doubt that the Macedonian fly fishermen mentioned by Aelian in A.D. 200 would take one look at a modern trout pattern and know instantly what it was for. Then they would ask you a lot of questions about how to tie it. One difference, however, cannot be ignored: the sheer number of different fly patterns available to the contemporary angler. This abundance of alternatives appears to be a fairly recent phenomenon, at least if the angling books of the past few hundred years can be taken as a reliable guide. Granted, not every pattern in use at the time was recorded in those older texts, but that's also true of flies and books today. By and large, anglers in previous centuries got along with far fewer patterns with less variety among them.

If forced to theorize on the basis of, at best, a patchy acquaintance with the written history of angling, I would say that an emerging preoccupation with fly patterns coincided roughly with the Industrial Revolution. In one sense, this is obvious; mechanization allowed for something like the mass production of hooks, tying tools, and some materials, making them more readily and widely available. A growing middle class had the means to purchase such things and the leisure to use them. There were simply more fishermen tinkering in the ways fisherman always do, which included tying flies. Less obviously, though, industrialization also brought with it a shift in outlook, a confidence in the application of scientific knowledge for the betterment of the world, a belief in technological solutions to problems of all kinds, from digging canals to housing inmates. This conviction has especially deep roots in America, which from its beginnings has been a culture of better mousetraps, a characteristic that for good or ill explains much of our history and present condition. In any case, by the end of the nineteenth century, even George Bernard Shaw—a man committed to the efficacy of "science" in some of its less savory forms (eugenics, for instance) and a critic profoundly at odds with the world—still had enough in common with his times to voice its prevailing assumption: "All problems are essentially scientific problems." Today, his assessment seems so self-evident that no one even bothers to utter it.

I bring this up at all because an artificial fly is, among other things, a technological artifact; it is manufactured, in the original sense of being made by hand. (Bait, by contrast, is nontechnological; hatchery fish can be either.) A fly pattern is, in theory at least, an engineered solution to a problem, and in the past three decades or so these solutions have multiplied at a rate somewhere between impressive and staggering. The fly-fishing industry has no doubt driven some of this growth, but by far the greatest share of it owes to amateur tiers who have no commercial stake in things. How this has come about is revealing. The primary cause of all this activity has been a kind of cross-pollination of ideas, techniques, and even approaches to insect imitation among and between fly tiers in the United States and Europe. And what has fueled this exchange is clearly digital technology, which, in its most influential form, the Internet, has greatly accelerated new developments of all sorts in tying. Like the mechanization of the nineteenth century, the information revolution of our own time represents both the expanded availability of commodities and a kind of faith—the same faith, in fact, that looks to technology to overcome problems. The mind-set of industrialization has carried over with a vengeance into the postindustrial world.

We believe in the efficacy of tools, devices, hardware, and systems to overcome obstacles, whether they involve treating disease, waging war, making a phone call, educating the young, or extending the shelf life of our lettuce—"better living through chemistry," as the saying once went. The proliferation of fly patterns reflects this same trajectory of thinking, and the pursuit of it with such vigor in an age that is—take your pick—

enamored with, obsessed by, worshipful of, dependent upon, or enslaved to technology could scarcely be called a coincidence. It probably couldn't have happened any other way. Nor is it an accident that much of the vigor in fly tying today comes from younger anglers who were born into this time.

It may seem far-fetched, but this notion of trout flies as the artifact and emblem of a technological world is validated by the trout themselves, or at least some of them. Since the beginning of the Industrial Revolution, many of the problems that called for solutions were created by industrialization itself, a feedback loop that has only intensified in the centuries since and has, in the last few decades, extended to trout streams. On some hard-fished rivers, particularly the popular tailwaters, trout can grow pattern-shy, resistant to what worked last year or last month or last week. So we devise ever-newer patterns to catch them, using fresh technological solutions to solve a problem created by former ones. It is exactly the same dance that takes place between data-security experts and hackers or between bacteria and antibiotics, for that matter, in which one can no longer distinguish cause from effect, action from reaction. It has often been suggested that a problem cannot be solved by using the same kind of thinking that gave rise to it in the first place, though I'm not sure that this matter can be easily or quickly decided. In fishing, as in the rest of our technological lives, the jury is still busy peer-reviewing proposals.

I don't suggest any of this as a specific indictment of modern fly fishing or anglers; it is merely a speculation, a theory to explain why trout flies—the object of fascination among anglers for many centuries—have such a particularly strong hold on the angling consciousness today. And in fact when it comes to fly patterns, I snap up new ideas as enthusiastically as the next person. While I have my doubts about technology in general, I seem to suspend them where trout flies are concerned. That the new patterns are not always to my taste is quite beside the point and, in a way, so is the question of whether they work better than what we already have. The search for the perfect fly is bound to produce mostly failures; that may simply be the nature of technological innovation. It certainly appears to be its method.

But in just the way that much of fly fishing, and most of what is best in it, exists apart from the mere mechanics of the sport, so a fly pattern is more than merely a product and symbol of technology. Whether we tie a fly or choose a pattern from a bin at the shop, we enlist it in a story of our own making. Our fly boxes tell a tale of what we believe we have learned—from our observations of fish and rivers, the inferences drawn from our own experiences, our conjectures about trout and water, and the provisional conclusions we have reached about them. A trout fly inhabits the space of our best imaginings and becomes a kind of narrative of its own, a plot we construct about a character in disguise. A fly pattern is a form of storytelling in the same way that a theory is the narrative of an idea. Certainly in the end we cast a fly on the water for the same basic reason that we test a hypothesis or read a story—we want to see how it all comes out.

9

LOCAL SEMIOTICS

As will be seen more clearly in a moment, all images are polysemous; they imply, underlying their signifiers, a "floating chain" of signifieds, the reader able to choose some and ignore others.

—Roland Barthes, "Rhetoric of the Image"

DRIVING FROM THE RANCH TO ENNIS TAKES ABOUT TWENTY-FIVE MINUTES, most of them spent skirting the foot of a bench at thirty-five miles per hour on a back road with no shoulders or painted centerline but plenty of patched asphalt, rutted gravel, and blind curves. It carries only local traffic, invariably light. In one direction, the road is seasonally impassable and heads to nowhere that cannot be reached by an easier route anyway. In the opposite direction, it leads to both supplies in town and fishing, so we end up traveling it often. And here in the valley, as in farm and ranch country nearly everywhere, it is the universal custom to exchange a brief wave with an oncoming driver as you pass. That you may be strangers, typically the case with us since we are "not from around here," as they say around here, means nothing. The wave is bigger than both of you, a fundamental idiom in the visual vernacular of rural America, as indigenous to the country byway as raising a middle finger or waving a firearm is to a freeway at rush hour.

In form, the gesture resembles the swiveling, disembodied hand of a perma-smile pageant queen about as much as West Yellowstone resembles Pasadena. Anyone who's driven the back roads knows it: four fingers of the hand gripping the top of the steering wheel are lifted and lowered in a continuous motion that literally takes less than a second. Minimalist and untheatrical, it epitomizes the kind of practical economy I associate with people who can repair their own tractors, install a well pump, deal with a bull, and generally get a job done without a lot of fanfare or unnecessary extras.

The probable origins readily suggest themselves, recalling a time when mostly local people traveled mostly local roads. The wave simply recognized a familiar face and perhaps earned a few crumbs of karmic goodwill, potentially redeemable later should you find yourself in a ditch with a blown tire and a broken axle. But the gesture has outlived those circumstances, and that it has persisted in a place annually overrun by transient anonymous outsiders makes the contemporary use of the sign more difficult to pin down. To call it a "greeting" seems somehow inappropriate to the context—two human beings in random passing at a combined velocity of seventy miles per hour—and to attribute it to some generalized friendliness overlooks its back-road particularity. You never see the wave delivered in a city or on the freeway, and in town it passes only between friends. The wave represents an acknowledgment of some sort, but of what specific sort I'm not sure. I appreciate its understated form; I commend its power to transcend the monadic enclosure of the modern automotive self-o-sphere; I am even drawn to the mysterious allegiance it presupposes. But its deeper structures remain unclear.

Uncertainties in interpretation frequently precipitate problems in protocol; you can be left wondering just what your participation in the wave might signify. The matter of who goes first, for instance, seems relevant, and I never grow more keenly self-conscious or ambivalent than when the license plate of an approaching car suggests that the driver might be a local. Mindful of how visitors like myself invade the place each summer, I worry that initiating a wave might be perceived as the overeager ingratiations of a tourist on holiday. Such people presume to a familiarity that does not exist and may force a return wave in a kind of extorted intimacy that leaves the other driver feeling he's been compelled to engage in a nonconsensual act. Or you might open yourself to the emotionally complicated possibility of getting no wave in return, perhaps intended as a deliberate snub, one of those calibrated gestures of resentment that an invaded people devise for their invaders. It could even communicate that you are despised beneath notice, intimating the subtextual hope that with enough unreciprocated waves you will go back to wherever you came from. On the other hand, responding only to a proffered wave could be construed as arrogance, the tourist's presumed superiority, an assumption of a hierarchical entitlement like the one governing military salutes. Regardless of how often you visit a place far from home, you never become fully naturalized; it always has its green-card aspects, and I no more wish to be seen as demanding a kind tribute than I do as making unwelcome advances.

Separate issues arise when a license plate reveals that the driver comes from out of state, a person much like yourself. This situation introduces the whole question of whether the wave is even appropriate or merely represents an empty mimicry or a clumsy imposture, like two American tourists in Tokyo bowing to each other. I suppose under these circumstances waving might signify the mutual recognition of strangers in a strange land, but it could also implicate you in a lame affectation and a wasted wave.

The gesture presents other hermeneutic indeterminacies. In a variant form, the oncoming driver raises only the index finger, and I am unsure whether this implies seventy-five percent less commitment to whatever is being signified or just expresses a personal style. More cryptic still is the driver who delivers a wave at the last possible instant, so that no matter how laserlike my own reflexes, the return wave goes unseen; he has already passed by. Maybe he became distracted and returned to himself too late for more than a tardy but well-intentioned attempt. Or possibly he considers me an asshole for not waving back, though I did and he didn't see it. It has even occurred to me on occasion that the approaching driver, disaffected and resentful of my presence on the road, deliberately contrived this exact reaction, delivering a late wave knowing full well the distress I would suffer at seeing myself being perceived as an asshole. This disturbing line of interpretation gains further support when the delayed wave comes in the low-energy, uninvested, one-finger version, a signal that with the slightest movement of a single digit—indeed he would not take more trouble—he could leave me feeling foolish, belittled, and misunderstood, waving in return at an empty road.

These are troubling ambiguities, and we talk of them at the ranch.

The back door of the house at the ranch opens onto a wooden porch elevated five steps off the ground, not a fatal drop but one worth avoiding, and so a railing built of two-by-fours surrounds the perimeter. Fastened to one of the top rails is a rectangular wooden flower box about four feet long. The planks have weathered with the years and warped a little, and the nailed butt joints have begun to separate at the corners. It still holds soil, though it hasn't contained flowers for quite some years, and even the windblown weeds that once sprouted in their place have been all but crowded out by a clutter of bits and pieces retrieved from the surrounding landscape, the kinds of things you might pick up when out walking or hiking or fishing and think worth the small effort of carrying back to show someone else.

A few of these items are manmade—a worn-out horseshoe; an old, pitted axe head; a fragment of decorative cast iron broken from a long-gone woodstove—but most come from the natural world. The planter holds dozens of rocks—chunks of milky quartz, shards of talc, agates, splinters of petrified wood, jasper, pieces of limestone embossed with fossils or encrusted in sugarlike crystals, river stones that look quite plain until rainwater brings out a hidden color or pattern or luminosity. A number of bones—the lower mandibles from a couple of deer, a few ribs and vertebrae, an intricate rodent skull with tiny amber-colored teeth, a short but thick femur of unknown origin, a fractured scapula—are jumbled together with pieces of antler, bits of wood that have been smoothed to interesting shapes by the river, and other such ordinary treasures. Scattered among these more durable artifacts are the seasonal ephemera of feathers, owl pellets, unusual seedpods or wild plants that disintegrate and blow away come winter.

No particular logic informs the assortment beyond that indiscriminate magnetism that draws some people to encounter a place on its smaller scales. Nor do the contents reveal any plan or premeditation in the collecting. The flower box simply accumulates these things in the same way that a beach house inevitably accrues shells and driftwood. Some of them have been put there by the Segals, who come out every summer for a month or two before our arrival, and some by us, particularly the Writer, the Painter, and the Bodhi, who find a special charm in such things. No effort has been made to keep the collections separate, and the contents change gradually as newer or more interesting specimens replace older or less appealing ones, though a certain propriety is observed. Not knowing what value the Segals might place on specific objects, we make these substitutions only among our own contributions, and though certainly no one keeps track, to all appearances they have in turn abided by the same principle. Perhaps, as the Painter maintains, this owes only to pure coincidence or my own faulty memory. But the world does not lack for signs. Granted, in reading them we are apt to find whatever we look for, as with dreams and horoscopes, yet it seems to me that this ongoing allocation of space in the planter does not merely acknowledge our yearly occupation of the ranch but after a fashion accommodates it even when we are not there. The flower box and its archive have come to represent a kind of tacit reciprocity between two groups of people who, in the course of twenty years, have never once met.

This is beyond question a minor and quite probably insignificant matter; I mention it at all because, over time, the planter appears to have become a vehicle of small mutualities in other ways. We may, for instance, arrive one summer to find that the Segals have added a new stone or bone unmistakably similar to one of our own or contributed some specimen that closely reflects our own collecting proclivities. On many occasions we've shown up at the house to discover some of the objects in the planter rearranged in unexpected or whimsical ways—stones assembled into miniature abstract sculptures; assorted bones loosely composed into some improbable skeleton; four or five feathers wedged into the pitted surface of a rock to form the fanlike tail of a surreal turkey; three ribs and a horseshoe formed into an archway over nothing. One summer we found that a small deer skull we'd left in the planter had a very ocular-looking geode—its white, spherical surface fractured to reveal a dark center—pressed into the eye socket. But the stone was a little too large and bulged hideously from the side of the head in a wild, accusatory stare, and in the unsettling way of some kitsch novelty paintings, the eye followed you around wherever you moved.

These collages and tableaux may simply represent nothing more consequential than a form of idle, three-dimensional doodling—undoubtedly that is the case—and each instance on its own seems trifling even as I record it. But I've always regarded them collectively and in the larger context of our cumulative trips to the ranch. I would scarcely claim that these arrangements were in any sense "put" there for us, but perhaps they were left there in a passing awareness that we would notice them, as we inevitably do, and find them mildly entertaining or even a little bizarre. Consulting the flower box early in our stay to see what changes have been wrought, the additions and subtractions and new configurations, has become a regular practice. As the weeks progress, we introduce our own revisions and amendments, presumably to be discovered when the owners return. Although I have no evidence whatsoever that these are ever noted, I have always imagined they are.

One can, as the Painter repeatedly cautions, read too much into all of this, gently hinting that hyperanalysis itself can signify a type of latent narcissism. But one can also, I insist, read too little into it; the act of creation is inseparable from that of interpretation. The alternating recombinations of items in the planter have begun to assume the attributes of some rudimentary form of discourse, each set of visitors reworking its contents—primarily for their own interest or idle amusement, but possibly also in the consciousness of a second, eventual audience in the background whose reactions are, if only distantly, envisioned or entertained. Nothing as direct or purposeful as a "message" is involved; the raw materials are too specialized to convey much beyond a sense of humor, a penchant for the fanciful, an inclination to the droll. Though their arrangements do not express an idea, they do register a sensibility, in itself a sufficiently delicate task.

This visual gesturing (or "alleged gesturing," as some would have it) does not confine itself entirely to the porch planter; articles inside the house participate at times and occasionally in a fashion that hints at a more explicitly conversational character. On a shelf in the kitchen, for instance, there has long stood an approximately life-sized, cobalt-blue, glass statuette of a young woman's hand, the slender fingers tapering upward. Some years back, the Bodhi brought with him a roughly similar figurine of glazed white porcelain, obtained, as I recall, at a flea market. With tubular, jointless digits pointing stiffly skyward from a featureless palm, it looks like a slightly inflated rubber glove, an unsurprising resemblance since it had functioned as a dipping mold to manufacture the latex surgical type. He put this hand on the shelf alongside the original one—a wry echo perhaps, or an ironic comment on the blurred boundaries between art and industry; I doubt the reason was clear even to him. The following year we discovered it embellished with a red, white, and blue crepe-paper wristband—patriotic shrapnel, I surmised, from the local Fourth of July celebration of a few weeks before. The summer after the Bodhi and the Intended were married, makeshift wedding bands appeared on the ring finger of each hand. And so on. I realize that this sounds trivial, but it must be multiplied several times over to get the aggregate effect, since small improvisations of this sort extended to other domestic objects and have continued, not in any methodical fashion but with the rhythms of ordinary talk, animated at times with silences in between.

None of this holds any great importance, perhaps none at all, and I'm uncertain of the significance, should there even be any, of these cryptic exchanges, if in fact they really constitute exchanges at all, which the Painter routinely assures me they don't, insisting that the whole thing is just in my head. But that, of course, is where all signification resides, possibly adjacent to that region of the brain responsible for willful misinterpretation. It is pointless to look for some encoded meaning in these extemporaneous compositions of physical objects; whatever meaning exists, I expect, lies more in the fact of their having been arranged than in the final form. And while I do not understand it, I have come to appreciate this curious species of visual rhetoric, its vocabulary of artifacts indigenous to the natural and domestic landscapes, its grammar of contiguity, and its syntax of juxtaposition. It is like conversing in a tongue that no one quite understands, the speech of rocks, the discourse of bones, and the strange articulations of the side-by-side.

Although the west entrance of Yellowstone National Park lies only an hour from the ranch, we do not make the trip often. The crush of people and squeeze of traffic along roadways clotted with abandoned cars, their owners having wandered off to get gored by the buffalo they're trying to pet, provide abundant discouragement. But from time to time we become stricken with guilty feelings of missed opportunity, a sense that we ought to go since we're so close, the way you feel that you really should use your gift membership to the gym at least once in a while. Because of the crowds, however, reaching the Lamar Valley, our favored destination and one of the most pleasing landscapes in the Park, can require hours of combat driving, and traveling there to fish for a day turns into an insufferably long ordeal.

So one August, as temperatures in the Madison Valley heated up and the fishing cooled down, we shoehorned several thousand mostly unnecessary pounds of camping gear into a couple of cars and set out to spend a few days with the cutthroats of the Lamar drainage, eventually pulling into the Slough Creek Campground just as someone else was pulling into the last available site. We continued up the road to Pebble Creek, where, to our enormous relief, we found exactly one open camping spot. Or so it appeared. I had read at some point during the drive—perhaps in a brochure acquired at the Park entrance or maybe on a posting at the campground itself, I can no longer recollect—that visitors in RVs, campers, or other self-contained units who leave their campsite for the day should also leave behind some indication that the spot is taken and so prevent others from inadvertently moving in: a rope across the entrance, or a sign, or some item of modest but recognizable value (I distinctly remember that last term being used) as a symbol of occupation—a lawn chair, for instance, or a couple of towels on a clothesline.

We parked in the vacant site and had just begun the substantial toil of unloading our stuff when we discovered in the exact center of the government-issue picnic table an ice scraper of the type used to clear car windshields—an exceptionally high-quality ice scraper, I should make clear, brand-new with a cushioned-rubber, ergonomically formed grip and a wide, cleanly beveled Lexan blade. I would imagine that, as ice scrapers go, this was an expensive one. Immediately a discussion commenced, and before long we were seated at the picnic table for what would become a protracted symposium on the question before us: Can an ice scraper be used to secure a campsite?

Since our party of five included two teachers, two who had taught in the past, and one who would soon enter the profession, we naturally defaulted to what academics do best, filling the void of actual facts with abstract principles and speculative inference. We are trained to this; I am not sure why, though naturally I have a theory. The Cook and the Bodhi, consistent with their temperaments, began at the beginning and took up the question from a more or less epistemological standpoint: What constitutes value? How do we know value, and wherein does it reside? And for whom? Is value intrinsic? If a thing can be of value to one person and worthless to another, does the concept of value itself have any objective validity? And if the concept is not shared, can the construct of value legitimately be used to signify anything? From there, we mucked a short distance into the sucking bogs of relativism, and then turned back.

The Writer and the Painter considered the scraper from the perspective of intentionality. Had it been left deliberately or accidentally? Was it a sign of something other than forgetfulness? Given the excessively warm weather, even at the higher altitudes of Yellowstone, it appeared unlikely that the ice scraper had been used, set down, and mistakenly left behind. They proposed that in light of the potentially meaningful centrality of its placement, its pristine condition, and its qualified claim to value ("Not intrinsic value, but *value for its kind*," the Writer carefully clarified), we should probably assume that some purpose lay behind the scraper, and that it might well signify the obvious—our spot had in fact already been claimed. ("However," the Cook insisted, "with no frost on the windshield, the ice scraper becomes functionless, without purpose—valueless, if our construction of value presupposes the fulfillment of a need or desire." But we had already moved beyond that.)

The Bodhi, having now taken up this new line of reasoning, developed a second interpretation: the scraper represented an indefinite signifier precisely because it was intended to accomplish one of two competing functions in what is ordinarily called playing both ends against the middle. Its owners, according to his conjecture, had gone to seek a campsite that would prove in some way more agreeable to them, and the scraper had been left as a contingency measure that would ensure them a place to stay for the night should their search prove unsuccessful. It wasn't, then, a question of relative value, that is, one depending upon the particular observer, but of conditional value, that is, of possessing worth or not to the same individual depending upon the circumstances. If a better place to camp could not be located, the scraper retained its value of symbolic occupancy; should new lodgings be found, it would become valueless, an object sacrificed in the acquisition of greater value and a dispensable stage prop in the daily campsite theatrics in the park.

These deliberations were mercifully interrupted by the appearance of a park ranger, who motored slowly through the campground and stopped at the site of dispute, presumably to find out why five people were sitting around an empty picnic table in the middle of August passing around an ice scraper. He listened to our dilemma and picked up the object in question, which he examined in detail. ("Never seen one quite this nice," he said, admiringly.) Wanting no more than to see all parties, ourselves especially but also including those not present, treated equitably in the matter, we looked to this veteran of park affairs for a swift and just ruling: either the scraper legitimately established a prior claim or it was okay to camp here and he'd back us up should a difference of opinion arise later. Instead, he hesitated and then began, albeit in a more streamlined fashion, to retrace some of the same philosophical ground we had already fruitlessly trampled.

We talked this over for at least fifteen minutes, during which he parried our direct questions ("What should we do?") and deflected our hypothetical ones ("What would *you* do?"). And then much to our surprise, rather than carry the ball, he elected to punt and declared the matter irresolvable, refusing to express an opinion either in his official capacity or as a private citizen and fellow decoder of signs in the world. He would admit only that our worst fears could conceivably come to pass: that the owners of the ice scraper would return in the evening (I imagined them, unfairly, growling up in some two-story mobile leviathan excreting a contrail of diesel fumes from its foul, chrome-plated anus) and demand our eviction after we'd put up tents and settled in comfortably, at which point I could foresee some argument, perhaps the park authorities becoming involved, and the beginnings of an unpleasant business. But evidently relieved to regard it all as a private matter, the ranger walked back to his car and drove off, oblivious or indifferent to the obvious lacunae in his training.

We eventually settled the practical side of the issue by asking, Did the scraper in its present context possess value, *as that term is commonly understood?* As a sign, was it unambiguous? And would its significance be universally recognized in the larger camping community? Our answers were, respectively, no, no, and no, and so we stayed. No one ever showed up, and so the truth of the matter was never revealed, nor were the theoretical issues at stake ever forced to conclusion.

When we left, I took the ice scraper and have kept it. It is a symbol of something or other.

One of the kitchen windows at the ranch looks out on the long, straight stretch of gravel road that passes by the house. The prospect is such that you might spot an approaching car a full mile away, though covering the distance will take it several minutes on the capriciously maintained road, where potholes and washboard make for slow travel. On those evenings when some of us are not due at the ranch until late, are coming back from fishing or shuttling someone to the airport or are arriving after a long day's drive from out of state, I find myself inventing excuses for a trip to the kitchen—a glass of water I do not want, a bite to eat I do not need—so that I might check to see if any headlights are drawing near. A quick glance will not suffice, since midway down its length the road dips below the line of sight for a time and conceals any evidence of an advancing vehicle. And so I'll watch until I'm assured that there's nothing out there and return to my book or the fly-tying vise, only to wander back a few minutes later and peer again out the window, beyond the glassy reflection of the lit room behind me, through the shadow of my own silhouette, and into the deep pitch of night. Every story has its dark edges, beyond which lie the parts untold and as yet peopled only with restive imaginings, the shadowy shapes of apprehension and expectancy, of relief and dread.

Now and then during these repeated circuits to the window, a car will appear far in the distance, flashing its high beams to spook a deer from the road, the headlights rising and falling as it bounces over the rough rock, dimming and brightening as it swerves around a deep rut, tracing a cursive of white light on a page of black glass, the strokes of a cipher written in disappearing ink. I lean closer to the window and strain to make out some familiar sign: the well-known slant of a misaligned headlamp, taillights on a boat trailer, a recognizable spacing or shape or tint of the beams—some clue to translating this optical telegraphy, some signal of safe return in this semaphore of light. For all stories rest in part on unraveling small encryptions of the ordinary.

10

SIRIUS MATTERS

Day after day, day after day,
We stuck, nor breath nor motion;
As idle as a painted ship
Upon a painted ocean.

> —Samuel Taylor Coleridge,
> "The Rime of the Ancient Mariner"

Midway along the journey of our life
I woke to find myself in a dark wood, . . .
How I entered there I cannot truly say

> —Dante, *Inferno*

AT A VISUAL MAGNITUDE OF -1.42, IN THE CONSTELLATION CANIS MAJOR, Sirius is the brightest star in the night sky, the shining eye of the Great Dog that trots at Orion's heels. From earliest times, astronomers have called it the Dog Star, and here in the middle latitudes, from early July until early September, Sirius rises and sets with the sun, as a great dog should. In Greek, the name means "burning" or "scorching," and since antiquity the Dog Star has lent its name to this middle part of the summer, the dog days. Our annual stay at the ranch always begins and ends during this interval.

Some years bring as well, however, a season within this season, a smoldering, incandescent stretch of days when the mercury flirts with triple digits and a string of nights not much cooler—the depths of the dog days and the hottest part of the hottest part of the year. The summer has reached the halfway point between its astronomical birth at the June solstice and its passing at the September equinox, and the season is showing signs of middle age. The fertile vitality of its youth, the vigorous green imagination that reinvented the landscape with every passing rain and every shower of sun, the grand inventions of sky that re-created themselves daily, the explosive ingenuity of change have all spent themselves and passed. The season appears to have run out of ideas, able only to repeat its middle-aged ways from one day to the next. The summer does less growing now and more just growing old, foreshadowing a foregone conclusion but still too distant from its own end to make out the fall. In the unvarying heat and haze, the world seems becalmed in the equatorial doldrums of midlife, stalled at an in-between time in a weatherless kind of weather. It feels a little tired, in need of a change but unable, for the life of it, to come up with anything new.

Instead, in the forge of each day, the sun hammers the landscape to the same hard and brittle sheet of earth. Every afternoon, a wind like a rush of oven air swirls billows of pulverized gravel, powdery soil, and bits of chaff through open windows and gaps in the door frame. A film of dust hangs in the air, and a mealy grit settles over the ranch, inside and out. With the humidity down into the teens, the Painter and the Mechanic suffer nosebleeds. You sweat without feeling it, a salty rime on your shirt back and collar the only evidence, as though the parched air sucked moisture directly through your skin without the intermediate step of perspiration. Sometimes, in the recent years of drought especially, the valley and mountains blur in the smoke of forest fires as far away as Missoula and

Flathead Lake. The sky glows a deep blood-orange; the air smells charred. And when the smoke clears out, the flame of sun seems to ignite the air itself; the day burns at both ends with a shimmering heat that can leave you feeling like a man made of wax.

On a day such as this we set out to drift a stretch of river that had the indispensable virtue of running among islands wooded with tall trees where we might find a little shade. There were three of us—the Bodhi and I and a companion I'd first met some thirty years prior, in the dun haze of a college dorm room, where my brother introduced him to me as Honchus-Lotus. I never understood how he came by the name, but the latter part of it does accurately evoke a soft-spoken thoughtfulness and natural equanimity that make him, in the way that some people manage, serenely at home wherever he happens to be. At the same time, he is an acute and ruthless critic of human absurdity, which he accepts with the droll cynicism of one who knows that the world will consistently live down to his expectations. It's an oddly hybridized sensibility, a cross of sorts between the Dalai Lama and Ambrose Bierce, and so some form of hyphenated name was probably inevitable.

Honchus-Lotus had arrived at the ranch the previous day, and since he does not make the trip every summer, a certain prodigal-son atmosphere always surrounds his return. We have much to catch up on, and in the course of the evening's celebration under the cottonwoods he revealed that he had, for the past year or so, been involved in a romantic association of the serious and potentially enduring sort. While Honchus-Lotus has, like the rest of us, reached middle life, he arrived there after a long and apparently contented bachelorhood, so his announcement occasioned surprise, toasts, and a great many questions. The Writer, it being in her nature, pressed for more details, which he supplied in a text-and-commentary format, loosely alternating between the specifics of his situation and larger observations about their meaning. At one point during this discourse, just as an aside, he noted that he'd spent a great deal of time contemplating men and women and the relationships between them and had thought about writing a book on the subject. The spontaneous outburst of hilarity made further conversation impossible for some long interval. When it at last subsided, the Painter wondered aloud, and rather tactfully I thought, whether a life largely spent single was really the kind of credential that qualified one for this particular kind of undertaking. Honchus-Lotus countered that what mattered most was how much you learned, not how long it took. "I have reflected on this a lot," he said, looking a little wistfully up at the evening sky. And when he presented the first three chapter ideas—"Obey All Instructions," "Lower Your Standards," and "Only One of You Has to Want to Get Married"—even the Painter was compelled to admit that certain key concepts had not been lost on him and that the project showed unusual commercial potential, especially for a first book, with a prospect of sales across the gender spectrum.

We talked of this and other matters as we drifted downriver in the mounting heat of the following morning, eventually pulling over to a familiar stretch of low, cobbled bank. The current here breaks around a stony point above, glances gently off the far bank, and fans out over a long pool below with such obliging uniformity that just about any cast at all placed in a general upstream direction results in a long, drag-free float of the type I've seen elsewhere only in hypothetical diagrams. Fishing this kind of water can get you believing that you're better than you actually are, and so it makes an ideal spot for an inexperienced angler. Like nearly everyone who fly-fishes, I have tried to teach others how to do it, in scenarios that ranged from offering the already budding zealot a few words of counsel to perpetrating forcible acts of fly fishing on the hesitant and unwilling. In some of the earliest episodes, I was little more than a beginner myself, the useless leading the helpless with a stunningly naïve unselfconsciousness. And I recall them with the kind of stabbing embarrassment you experience at seeing yourself in an old home movie, cavorting about in polyester bell-bottoms back in the days when darkness descended on the land and disco strode the earth in platform soles, thick and terrible. Chastened by those memories, I've grown more cautious.

But Honchus-Lotus had asked me to show him a few things, and I knew he would make a willing and easy student, having already advanced from square-one beginnerhood into the early novice phase. He had some basic skills, a quiet enthusiasm, and, perhaps extrapolating from affairs of the heart, reduced expectations. I stationed him along this perfect pool, offering him a pointer or two about casting and a little advice about fishing the water. Just before heading downstream, I gave him two or three other flies and suggested that if the original pattern failed to get results, he might try one of the alternatives. These he took in the palm of his hand and examined for a moment, stirring them around with an index finger like a man sorting through pocket change, and then asked, "How do I know if the fly I've got on isn't working?" I pointed out that not catching anything might be taken as a reasonably good preliminary indication. He said that he'd figured that part out for himself but was wondering how long that would be. "Should I fish it for fifteen minutes or an hour? Should I cast it twenty times or a hundred? How do I know when it's time to change?"

I had to think about this for a minute, and the longer I thought about it, the longer I kept thinking about it. In one sense, the question doesn't really have an answer, yet in another sense, every angler eventually answers it. You cannot describe to someone else that threshold of declining confidence below which you start shopping around in your vest. The point at which the necessity for change makes itself felt does not exist in the angling circumstances but in the angler; it is not a technical matter but a human one, with all the variation that implies. At one extreme are the glacially patient, who believe that if they just hang with an idea long enough, just keep on doing what they do, things will eventually work out. At the opposite end are those perpetually engaged in the search for a better way, changing what and how and where they fish, looking for the winning combination or trying to force some action on a slow day. It isn't a question of one type of fisherman being more successful or persistent than the other; I've known excellent anglers of both kinds, and each tendency speaks to its own brand of perseverance.

But the noniconoclastic majority of us fall somewhere in that large middle territory along the continuum between patience and adaptability, generally inclining one way or the other but in some measure ambidextrously resourceful. Thoreau says we fish the waters of our own nature, and the particular way we balance the two attributes shapes a part of our angling identities because it forms a part of our nonangling ones. The negotiation, though, never ends and, as in other ways that we engage the world, will change with the circumstances or with the years. If any pattern exists, I'd venture that those who've spent their share of decades fly fishing, or simply their share on the planet, lean a little more to the side of patience. The capacity for it appears to grow naturally with age, in part, frankly, because you no longer quite have the juice to be actively impatient, which is strenuous, or don't react and adjust with the readiness you once did, or believe you once did. As the years pass, it seems not only wiser but easier to stand pat than to change. When it comes time to adapt to circumstances, you trust that you can rally to the occasion, though you'd prefer not to test this proposition with any regularity. But you cannot describe to someone else when patience becomes meaningless obstinacy or a species of fear, just as you can't isolate the precise moment when constant retooling amounts to indecision and self-doubt. And so I told Honchus-Lotus about the only thing I could: to trust whatever mechanism he normally relies on to detect futility in any of its many forms, then change flies. He seemed to know what I meant.

I continued to ponder his question, however, for another and less abstract reason. Days of blistering heat had driven the trout into a sulk, and finding a way to improve their mood had risen to a matter of some urgency and much speculation at the ranch. A trip of any real duration, of course, almost inevitably suffers a period of slow fishing, sometimes more than one. And generally, bright, hot August days account for some of the slowest, although rivers that originate in the high-altitude snows of the Rockies do fare somewhat better than those in other places, where streams warm to bathwater after midsummer. On the Madison in particular, the effects of dog-day heat are mitigated to a degree as the river passes through Hebgen Dam, which cools the water and can, at least theoretically, meter it out to stabilize the flow over the summer months.

Damming a river, however, automatically invokes the law of unintended consequences. I have never seen it work otherwise. In the first place, during the increasingly hot, dry, fire-prone summers of recent years, many of southwest Montana's best-known trout rivers have been shut down to angling—too little water that is much too warm for the fish to survive the fishermen, or in some cases just survive at all. With its more favorable water conditions, the Madison has so far remained open to anglers, and the pressure on it has accelerated. Guides from other places bring their clients; do-it-yourselfers on vacation, evicted by stream closures elsewhere, frequently end up here. Moreover, a dam represents little more than a concrete stopper with a faucet, and once you install the plumbing, everyone wants to control the tap to his best advantage. It is the enduring theme of the history of the West. The dam operators, particularly in the drought years, work with any number of loaded pistols pressed to their skulls by various claimants to the shrinking supply of water. And uppermost in the mind of these unfortunate hostages isn't what's best for the fish but which particular trigger finger is the most impulsive. Anglers, outfitters, fish biologists, environmentalists, and just normal people who love rivers also hold a gun of their own, but they haven't yet managed to acquire any bullets. So water releases are "managed" in ways that bounce the river level up and down with what appears to the angler as unfathomable caprice.

I have never heard a satisfactory explanation for why these fluctuating water levels reverberate through the fishing to such striking effect. On occasion, a flush of cool water will perk up the trout, which makes sense. Most of the time, however, whether the water rises or drops or the temperature goes up or down, the fish respond the same way, becoming out of sorts and uninclined to bite. Certainly, changes in river height push the trout around to some degree, as low water shrinks their living space and high water enlarges it again. At the same time, aquatic insects probably behave in much the same way, as they evacuate and recolonize the shallow margins of the stream. One might plausibly infer that all this moving back and forth would promote more frequent encounters between trout and bugs, and the fishing would pick up. But as often proves the case with trout, one would be wrong, at least about the second part. I sometimes wonder if the fish may in fact be reacting to the absolute amount of water in the stream rather than its depth. On this relatively broad river, an increase or reduction of water flow, even by as much as twenty-five percent, produces a comparatively modest rise or fall in water level, measured in inches rather than feet. Perhaps these variations register on some pressure-sensing mechanism, akin to the one that responds to barometric conditions, although this conjecture doesn't explain much, such as why fish should care about water- or air-pressure variations in the first place. Maybe trout, like anglers, are just inclined to resist change regardless of its nature.

Nevertheless, when the water level begins to jump around, as it will most every August, and a spell of intense heat hits, as it sometimes does, the fishing, like the weather, can go to the dogs. If the trout shut down suddenly, you might spend a couple of days pretending that it's only a passing lull—which happens even in the best of times—and you rig up every morning with the cautious hope that, today, things will get back on track. The residual inertia of this delusion becomes particularly powerful when the trout have been looking up and taking dry flies, which produces the most congenial state of affairs in all of fly fishing and so the one surrendered most unwillingly. And should the dog days descend in a good grasshopper year when the big fish come to the top and even sloppy casting provokes abusive, cyclonic strikes, you may fish on in denial for some time, incapable of accepting the truth that the magic fly of a few days before no longer works its juju. The hoppers are everywhere, and the trout should be feasting on them, and it is simply impossible for you to believe that they are not, despite the confirmations of your own experience, which repeat themselves with every cast, or approximately once every fifteen seconds over the course of an entire day, or days. The echo of recent success still resonates too audibly, and that you cannot stop listening plunges you into self-defeating recidivism. You throw the same ineffectual solutions at the same intractable problem to the same vain end, like a program sponsored by the federal government.

Eventually, you force yourself to admit that what you're doing isn't working and that if you keep on doing it, it's just going to keep on not working. But before resigning yourself to circumstances and making a change, you find yourself wishing for change to come to you—for a cloudy day if it has been bright, a clear one if it's been smoky; for the rain to start; for the temperature to go up or down; the river to rise or fall—any change at all, you think, would have to improve matters. What you are actually wishing for, of course, is better fishing, though putting it to yourself in these terms too obviously lays bare its essential improbability. Like the wish to be rich or to be young again, it confronts you mainly with a sense of naked preposterousness. It feels wiser to disguise the fantasy in something more realistic, something that could actually happen, like a little change in the weather that could give the fishing a lift. But when Sirius wanders in, circles once around southwest Montana, then lies down, curls up, and goes to sleep, the smothering weight of heat and airborne dust cannot be wished away. I number these among the least habitable days of the inhabitable narrative, a recurring leitmotif that grows heavier the longer it hangs around. The story of your fishing has nowhere to go because the main characters refuse to speak. Back at the ranch, there are iced drinks all around and much talk of the weather.

We have no fixed protocols or default backup plans when the fishing turns off like this. From time to time we poke around farther upstream to see how matters stand there. A comparatively large and long river like the Madison will sometimes exhibit inconsistencies, one section fishing reasonably well while another stretch ten miles away is funereally slow. It has nothing to do with localized hatches or an infusion of cold water from a tributary or anything so obvious. I have no idea at all what accounts for this kind of variation and just accept it as another one of the many things I have never understood about fishing. But such disparities, at least on a scale worth bothering about, do not occur regularly nor do they last long, and browsing around the river mainly involves just another attempt to sell yesterday's flies to yesterday's trout, to hunt up those few fish who still share your worldview or haven't yet gotten word that the bite is off. So we tend to stay with the familiar ten- or fifteen-mile stretch of river that we normally fish, figuring, or at least humoring ourselves, that knowing the water counts for more than anything when a general downturn in conditions forces layoffs in the catching department.

What emergency countermeasures we do take run the gamut, but in recent years especially we have resorted to a method known at the ranch as "slapping the hamster," though in fact it just describes a style of streamer fishing long popular on Rocky Mountain rivers and familiar to nearly everyone who fishes the Madison. The flies, alleged to imitate sculpins, baitfish, young trout, or leeches, reach imposing dimensions in a crude form of taxidermy involving rodent pelts and a four-inch hook. Sometimes, they are smartened up with festoons of twinkling prismatic ribbon, assorted holographic doodads, and, at the front, a gleaming brass bullet that always puts me in mind of Tycho Brahe's nose. We fish these flies mainly from the boat, in approved western fashion. The hamster makes a large-bore and formidable piece of ordnance, especially when it gets wet and heavy. In the interests of public safety, it is best delivered with a high, lifting backcast and an authoritative forward punch, usually into eddies and coves and undercuts along the bank. You can't really present a projectile of this sort with any degree of refinement. It hits the water like a sack of sand, and the angler, trained to attribute purpose to what is merely unavoidable, theorizes that such commotion "gets the trout's attention." This much could hardly be otherwise. The fly is then retrieved in brisk, staccato strips that replicate the movements of a living baitfish about as credibly as the fly imitates its appearance.

The selection of pattern never appears to be critical, though we all have our darlings. Mine purports to be a sculpin, spun of olive fur and manicured to a roughly teardrop shape, with flaring pectoral fins behind a wide head. It is not a fly I tie well, and my rendition, viewed head-on, more closely resembles a miniature chimpanzee with hideously large ears. On those infrequent occasions when he can be persuaded to relinquish his dry flies and truss up a hamster, the Photographer favors a bunny-leech affair with a big gold bead at the head that, when dripping wet and hanging from his leader, looks like a little mouse wearing a deep-sea diver's helmet. The Cook, the Bodhi, and the Mechanic will pretty much fish whatever someone hands them. Keenly attuned to impending calamity, the Painter prefers not to be in the boat when the hamster follies are in progress.

Anglers most commonly resort to this method during the fall, when large brown trout begin to develop the kyped jaw and bad attitude they will carry into spawning season. Miraculously, however, it will sometimes turn fish during the dog days when more genteel approaches ring up nothing. The flies have the added benefit of hooking bigger-than-average fish, the smaller ones presumably scattering in terror. A dynamic and industrious form of fishing, it requires constant casting, retrieving, and twitching of the rod tip. On slow days, all of this activity produces the illusion that you are actually doing something, energetically involved in improving your fortunes rather than just surrendering to the essential passivity of dead-drift fishing. On the other hand, it can get wearying, and when the arm flags and the mind wanders, mistakes can be made—a mistimed cast, an inadvertent body piercing, possibly tetanus or someone losing an eye. It does not make for elegant fishing, but at some point this ceases to matter. Even on the best of days, however, the strikes hardly come one right after another, and under the heat lamp of an August sun, they often don't come at all. Hamster slapping does not appeal to all tastes, nor to mine most of the time, but when the trout grow sulky and apathetic, I get a little less choosy about how I go after them.

Or a lot less when circumstances require it. One effect of the dog days is that they force you to face the lengths you will go to in order to catch fish, in much the way I imagine the Donner party was forced to contemplate mealtimes. While not true of all rivers, or always true of the Madison, and while fly anglers dislike confronting the fact, often enough the uglier the method, the better it works. And though I make my way to the gutter with reluctance, I do ultimately end up there and some days turn to deep nymphing, which begins as ordinary nymph fishing but steadily deteriorates in direct proportion to both the number of split shot you strap on and the weight of desperation they represent. The setup is gloomily familiar: a point fly and a single dropper, Montana law mercifully forbidding the misery of a second; more split shot than you'd confess to in polite society; and a strike indictor sufficiently muscular to counteract the aggregate weight of everything else, all strung along ten or twelve feet of leader. Even done skillfully, flinging this necklace of stuff all day is like swinging a pick, and its general resemblance to hard-rock mining does not escape you. Done poorly, it is like hurling a small galaxy out into space, each of its tethered planetary bodies in complex, orbital gyration around the others, a four-ball bolo bound for catastrophe that unfolds in slow motion before your eyes. I have no moral qualms at all about this kind of draglining and steer clear of the debates over whether it legitimately constitutes fly fishing or merely entails fishing with a fly on tackle poorly contrived to resemble spinning gear. During the dog-day lull, the distinction seems particularly precious and irrelevant. I do have my standards but prefer to maintain them when the fishing is better.

In more youthful summers, I possessed an enthusiasm and capacity for this brand of nymph fishing that I can scarcely believe now. I suppose, like everything else when I first moved to the West—the landscape, my life—it presented me with a fresh opportunity. It also put me into trout, far more of them than I deserved, for I never became much good at indicator fishing, which is another thing I can scarcely believe, considering how much time I once spent at it. But the endless fidgeting with weight and depth, the casting tangles of theological complexity, the evitable error inevitably made of squeezing on just one more split shot to get a little bit deeper, and the endless rerigging after snags—all of these I accepted gladly and without question. It was, after all, fishing, at least of a sort. Over the years, though, I grew increasingly unable to ignore its laborious, minimum-wage feel, like a job but without the dental coverage. And now only on the slowest days will I consign myself to this form of toil, its charmless mechanics and potential for tragedy, its dreary metaphysic.

The Photographer, though superbly accomplished in the technique, can no longer abide the sight of it, and should I happen to scrape a trout off the bottom with a big weighted nymph, he reacts as though I've just Cloroxed the hole. The Mechanic, on the other hand, was born to go deep and fishes in the spirit of the most successful anglers I have known—those people who will stop at nothing. Being primarily a steelhead fisherman only encourages his reckless tendencies, foremost among them gandy-dancing into the turbulence until the current upstream pillows to his armpits, clamping on a string of sinkers with enough throw weight to stun a bison, and sounding the heavy water. On more than one occasion, while fishing below him and intent on changing flies or replacing a tippet, I have looked up to see the Mechanic bobbing past me in a semireclined float, his baseball hat dripping but intact, rod held crosswise in both hands above the water, looking vaguely as though he's driving a sulky. When he manages to hold his footing, however, he derricks up all manner of curiosities—rusted bits of tackle, scraps of fencing, fathoms of old monofilament, knots of bright orange baling twine—and these give a glimpse into a secret interior of the river that the dry-fly vendor, selling his trinkets on the surface, never sees. There's a lot more down there than you might imagine.

The most predictable result of this type of ditch digging, however, arrives in the form of whitefish, a species dismissed by the trout angler as a self-explanatory letdown. While the state of Montana officially classifies whitefish as a gamefish, few anglers view them in such an expansive light and instead write them off as an unfortunate embarrassment, a nuisance, a blighted moment of hope on the end of your line. In the combat zone of the modern American trout stream, whitefish are inconvenient civilians caught in the line of fire, at best a regrettable collateral damage, at worst a simple waste of ammunition, but either way the western angler's chief metaphor for disappointment. At one time, some fishermen routinely threw whitefish up on the bank to perish, out of disgruntlement or some warped conceit that they were ridding the river of "trash fish." And if there's any justice, such people are destined for a special circle of hell, there to be hectored for all eternity by mimes and Liza Minnelli impersonators.

The angler complains that whitefish don't jump, an inconsistently applied criterion since many trout don't either, and a pretty arbitrary one to begin with. Nor, he contends, do whitefish fight well, which must be conceded, up to a point. On a long line, a whitefish does put up the struggle of an overripe banana, but only because it reserves its most determined efforts for the moment you bring it to hand, when it suddenly unleashes a slithering whirlwind of uncontained fury that often makes releasing a whitefish the most difficult part of catching one. And they are, the argument continues, a drab and uncomely species. From an aesthetic viewpoint trained to trout, there may be some truth here; with a suckerlike face and mouthparts, a pilchard-shaped torso, and the forked tail of a herring, a whitefish does look a little like it is assembled from spare parts and slightly ashamed of it. Yet the grayling, a biological cousin and a fish much revered, does not materially differ in appearance. Where one man finds reasons, of course, another may see only rationalizations, and behind these allegations, I believe, lies the whitefish's one, true, and unforgivable offense: that it exists incompatibly with our wishes. Its crime consists of simply not being a trout.

This is a little harsh and in certain respects just splitting hairs. Whitefish belong to the same zoological family, Salmonidae, as trout; they occupy the same habitats, behave in distinctly troutlike ways, and take a fly equally well. Whitefish swam in Montana rivers long before Montana was ever invented, and they continue to thrive while other native gamefish, the cutthroats and bull trout and grayling, have been outcompeted, displaced, or eaten into extinction or near extinction in many places. If nothing else, whitefish are durable, which should not be underestimated in our environmentally calamitous times. By any objective accounting, whitefish ought to be more popular. On the one hand, in an age that talks much, though admittedly does little, about the preeminence of indigenous salmonids, their pedigree alone should entitle them to a certain prestige. On the other hand, for the underground fly-angling subculture that invests traditionally inferior species—carp, sharks, gar—with a certain hip, slumming-it cachet, the whitefish would seem a natural. Yet it enjoys neither the elder-statesman celebrity of its lineage nor the popularity of a thrill from the bad-boy side of the tracks. Theoretically, the species has a lot going for it, but it has never caught on. And so whitefish take their place alongside those other mysteries in life that appear to be conceptually sound, that in the abstract should work, but that in their concrete embodiments fail to function—the Environmental Protection Agency, for instance, any number of Microsoft products, and every committee I have ever served on.

As with the inferior orders in any hierarchical system, whitefish suffer the belittlement of derisive nicknames: "Montana bonefish," "snouts," "silver suckers," and so on. Decades ago, whitefish came to be known at the ranch as "whitedogs" or just "dogs," and while I can no longer reconstruct the reason, the name affords a certain convenience. When a partner forty yards downriver and tight to a fish looks your way, cups his hand to his mouth, and hollers, "Woof," you know that you can return to your own fishing without missing anything important. But more to the point, insofar as "dog" summons up both "contemptible cur" and "man's best friend," it accurately captures the more complex relationship that lurks beneath the fisherman's facile and disingenuous contempt for the species. The modern fly angler who catches a whitefish almost certainly pretends to a greater disappointment than he actually feels. I will grant him a mild chagrin but at the same time find it hard to imagine that anyone with angling in his soul would regret catching a fish, at least as opposed to not catching one. I would even go further and say that hooking a whitefish, especially when others haven't, confers a form of minor satisfaction, perhaps even low-grade pride, though one best kept concealed. That the angler will not merely endure but participate in some jesting at his own expense brings us closer, I believe, to the more complicated bond that exists between the angler and the whitefish, not in spite of the latter being a lesser species but precisely because of it. If an aversion to the whitedog doesn't fully square with our angling nature, it does with our human one. You may not like whitefish much, but you need them. They are necessary, answering a call from those murky sectors of the heart that are best left unexplored. For to grant the whitefish the esteem it deserves would deprive fly fishing of something indispensable to all human endeavors: a laughingstock, a buffoon, a comic foil—that which elevates our own efforts by virtue of being beneath them. A trout inspires admiration, even humility, and that is all well enough. But you can feel superior to a whitefish, and that is irreplaceable.

In the wilting heat of August, we need them even more, if not for themselves, then for the reassurance they offer that at least something down there still cares about eating. I don't really know if dogs bite better during the dog days or not—I rather doubt it—but it seems so. In the absence of trout, even the ordinary number of whitefish looms disproportionately large in a day's fishing, and so perhaps I associate them more closely with the high-summer doldrums than the actual case probably warrants. At the same time, they do appear somewhat less put off by the scorching weather, and I can recall, with a not altogether welcome clarity, a few blistering August days when the hounds were afoot and we caught them by the dozens, though in the trout angler's construction of things this still counts as poor fishing. Part of it was just luck—good or bad, depending on how you feel about whitefish—and part owes to their somewhat greater tolerance in the matter of presentation. A whitedog will more readily hit a dragging fly than will a trout, and with the weight of the flies and the split shot, the height of the water column, its differing current speeds, and the resistance of the indicator, drag becomes an almost chronic condition of deep nymphing even if anglers prefer to believe otherwise. Then, too, whitefish will, far more than trout, congregate locally in certain pockets of deeper water. Some of these dog pounds are well known to us, and on a slow day we have no reservations about stringing up a pair of small nymphs, loading on the lead, and shamelessly excavating these holes under the pretext of having caught a few trout in them before. But mostly we just wish to remind ourselves of the simple, animal pull that lies at the heart of the game.

Like ecologists, anglers have their indicator species, the resident seismographs that register fishing activity. Whitefish have become ours, and some years when the heat wave drags on, even the dogs stop biting, a signal that matters have officially become grave. We continue fishing, though we may shorten up the days a bit; not catching anything can be remarkably exhausting. As the various groups of anglers who have trooped off for the day return to the ranch, the labored unloading of a car or boat, the trudge of feet up the wooden porch stairs, and the weary thud of gear bags on the floor of the utility room all make it clear that no one has done much better than anyone else, that once again today has been a lot like yesterday. The afternoon debriefings around the kitchen table grow shorter. It does not take much time to summarize bad fishing. We are concerned but not defeated, and the doleful state of affairs on the river never seriously intrudes into the good spirits and compensatory pleasures at the ranch. Someone, probably the Intended—who does not fish but in her large and generous heart senses the general letdown—will all at once declare that, what with the heat and such, it must be Margarita Day, and the rest of us straighten up in our chairs and look at one another and wonder how we could have been so forgetful. A great bustling search begins for triple sec and the right kind of salt. The kitchen comes alive with the smell of freshly squeezed limes, various opinions concerning optimum proportions, and the chiming of ice in sweating glasses, after which we adjourn to the shade of the cottonwoods out back to clear our heads.

After a decent and sociable interval in which we distance ourselves enough from the days' events to reflect upon them objectively, our fishing circumstances are then revisited. Someone, probably the Cook or the Mechanic—who consider themselves uncommonly rational and systematic thinkers—will begin to dissect our angling predicament and sort through it piece by piece, examining each component individually to see if we have overlooked or ignored something critical. Tequila logic can make a dull instrument for this kind of autopsy, but it occasionally produces some novel insights. No matter where this takes us, however, we always remain sufficiently circumspect to tiptoe around the obvious: that it might, finally, be just too miserably hot and bright to catch anything at all. Instead, our deliberations begin with the premise that the fish are catchable. Though by no means self-evident, this assumption must be granted. What other choice do you really have? Admitting the contrary concedes in advance the essential futility of it all. Whether you ultimately hook any fish doesn't matter, but the possibility of it must exist. That alone gives meaning to your efforts, even the failed ones. And so after days of being roughed up by the heat and wind and water with nothing to show for it but a deepening perplexity, you still strike out each morning with the necessary supposition that you face a solvable problem.

The question that remains is whether or not you possess a solution. The nonfisherman reasonably supposes that what most demoralizes an angler is not catching any fish, and I imagine that for some this holds true; each man to his own dismay, I say, and it's impolite to criticize. But most anglers understand that magnificent days can be spent on a river with never a trout to hand. Far more troubling, I believe, is to find yourself deep in the dog days, flogging a resistant world whose underlying principles you apparently no longer grasp. Patience, it seems, will not solve the problem, though you could be wrong about this. Your personal history has proved little help. You've worked all the moves you know, tried the things you do well, the ones you do badly, and even a suspicious few you have read about but never before resorted to because you thought them phenomenally stupid, as they indeed turned out to be. You have no notion of where to go from here.

This may be among the most dispiriting of all human conditions: not failing to succeed—this much you can gracefully accept—but reaching in for something else and coming up empty-handed, arriving at the point where you have run out of ideas. You find yourself unprepared for this because you seem to remember always coming up with them in the past. At midseason, great vacancies sometimes appear. And it is profoundly dislocating, this sense of being unsynchronized with the present, of trailing the curve, of feeling perhaps a little old before what you have always presumed to be your time, though it occurs to you now that you never actually sat down and worked the numbers. There is a temptation to give it up and go home, nurse the ache that you've noticed of late in your casting shoulder, maybe share a glass of solace with a friend and talk wistfully of good old yesterday or, if matters grow extreme, play a round of prescription-bottle checkers, winner takes all.

Yet somehow you wish to stay in the game, don't feel quite ready to check into the Ride-A-Wee Home for Precociously Senescent Anglers and sign up for assisted shuffleboard. The search continues for some conceptual wedge to tap into the underside of the brain and shim the mind plumb. Standing midstream in a middle-aged season, waist-deep and spectacularly clueless, you shuffle randomly through your alternatives over and over, like a disillusioned spiritual seeker trying to pick a new religion from the yellow pages. But everything remains resolutely uncommunicative. Beneath it all rests the crucial assumption that your situation is not irresolvable, and you must now face up to its inevitable corollaries: first, that a more resourceful person with more imaginative ideas, perhaps even yourself not all that many years back, would resolve it; and second, that you do not appear to be that person. Clearly, something needs to be different, a change is highly indicated, and you would gladly make it but cannot, for what feels like the life of you, think of what to do. And you find yourself peeking over the edge of your own ineffectuality and bewilderment and wondering if voids are really as empty as people say. Possibly something will occur to you when the dog days end, or they will end when something occurs to you, and of course, you think, to be standing on a trout stream in the first place must be reckoned good fortune. Still, it is disheartening not knowing where to turn, becalmed at the middle latitudes in a weatherless kind of weather, lost and out of ideas, with "Nothing to eat," as Auden writes, "and nowhere to sit down."

Then one afternoon, to every appearance like all the others, without warning, clouds begin to mass above the Tobacco Root Mountains in the distance, unassumingly at first, then thickening and darkening and roiling forward in swelling bulbs of smoky gray lit within by jagged filaments of orange lightning. They push ahead of them a fresh breeze that grows cooler as it gathers speed and sweeps over the benches in gusts that flatten and lift the range grass in flashing waves, driving out the heat of the day as a ceiling of thunderheads unrolls and covers the valley in a quilted underside of ashy violet and indigo. Dusk descends before its time, and the first rain falls, not drops but immense, spattering gobbets of water that slap the roof and siding shingles and the trees outside, so loud that you cannot tell at first, just from the sound, when they've frozen to pellets of hail, hurled on sheets of ice-chilled wind and clattering through the leaves, clanking the rain gutters, rattling the windowpanes likes snares on a glass drum, bouncing off the hoods of cars parked outside, pelting the waders hung out to dry, shoveled by the wind into grainy drifts against doors and fence posts. Then as suddenly as it began the hail gives way to a squally rain, deafening cascades driven by downdrafts that shear dead limbs from the cottonwoods and tumble them across the grass into windrows along the fence, while thunder boils low overhead, chattering the picture windows in their frames and shaking the glass in the cabinets. And through it all comes the wild hiss of wind-lashed trees, a sound like breaking surf, as a furious beauty spins around, and over, and then away, leaving only a quiet shower that finally ends in the small hours of the morning.

Day dawns to an immaculate bowl of cobalt sky, scrubbed by wind and rinsed by rain, and the smell of damp earth carried on effervescent air, and the promise of fishing ahead.

Life is an odd duck. I have never understood the weather there.

11

It Is a Good Day to Drive

Longing, we say, because desire is full of endless distances.
—Robert Hass, "Meditation at Lagunitas"

IN THE LATTER STAGES OF THE FUNCTIONAL ETERNITY IT TOOK ME TO finish school, I enrolled in a seminar on American writers of the Great Depression era. At the time, I knew nothing about the literature of economic catastrophe and now know only slightly more. In the signature trajectory of my education, I got sidetracked, veering off the main thoroughfare of American letters when I happened across some of the books produced by the Federal Writers' Project. The Writers' Project, along with the Federal Art Project and the Federal Music Project and a few others, formed one arm of Roosevelt's ambitious national employment program, the Works Progress Administration. Much like the Civilian Conservation Corps, whose monuments to youthful energy and hard currency are still visible around the country, the WPA sought to help the nation back to its feet by paying ordinary citizens to fill jobs that the government essentially invented for them, mostly constructing bridges, roads, public buildings, and things of that sort. The Writers' Project, however, proceeded from the assumption, still novel today, that writers actually do perform work, at least theoretically speaking. But then, as now, most of them lacked any alternative marketable skills, and so in what must have been a gleeful and disbelieving moment, they were hired to write. It remains an encouraging confirmation for the rest of us that unemployed writers and government money can both be usefully occupied, though apparently only under conditions of duress.

The program had, if only briefly in some cases, a number of distinguished participants, among them Richard Wright, Ralph Ellison, Saul Bellow, John Cheever, and John Steinbeck. In a classic instance of the federal misallocation of resources, however, the Federal Writers' Project produced no fiction. Most of the work, in fact, has long been forgotten, and I'm told that much of what came from the arts programs generally—manuscripts, paintings, interviews and oral histories, sound recordings—languishes in crates, unarchived and even unopened, warehoused in some forgotten basement inside the Beltway. But one of the most visible and successful projects was the American Guide Series, a collection of travel handbooks covering the forty-eight states. Even today, these volumes provide some wonderful reading, not only for their glimpses into America of the 1930s—without interstate highways, Kwik-E-Marts, or drive-through indigestion from the ubiquitous American gut bomb—but also for their flashes of energy, life, wit, and irony as formerly jobless writers were turned loose on a country that, even during the Depression, had its droll aspects. At times, amid its more workmanlike duties, the writing expresses an authentic passion for place, an affection for a city or town or the exhilaration of a landscape, as though the writer had maybe once lived there.

Even at the time of my seminar, nearly thirty years ago, a great many of the particulars contained in these guides were outdated and the books themselves no longer in print. I gathered what few volumes I could locate, and one of them turned out to be the guide to Montana. As with all the books in the series, this one opened with an account of the geography, history, culture, and economics of the state. But the bulk of it consisted of driving tours along the various highways, each route keyed to a reference map, with commentary on the landscape and points of interest in a town-by-town format. The bigger cites, Butte and Bozeman, were accorded a dozen or so pages apiece, while the more numerous, smaller places merited only a sentence or two, such as this one:

> ENNIS, (4,927 alt., 400 pop.), a typical western village of wide streets and one-story frame buildings, is shaded by the abrupt bulk of Fan Mountain and in summer by its own willows, alders, and poplars. It was named for William Ennis, who came to Bannack (Grasshopper Gulch) in 1863, and later homesteaded on this site.

And then these words to the traveler heading up the Madison Valley to West Yellowstone on what was then State Highway 1:

> On the west the Tobacco Root Mountains, deeply green on slope and summit, shelter the valley; to the east the Madison Range lifts its amethyst tops into the sky. The slate-colored Gravelly Range, near the southern end of the route, resembles vast banks of flowing sand. . . . The route as a whole traverses one of the best fishing areas in the Northwest.

I'd read about Montana before, mostly in outdoor magazines and mostly about Yellowstone country, but never anything quite so systematic or that attempted to convey the impression of a place in quite the same way, with both its broad strokes and details communicated from the vantage point of its roads. I passed many hours tracing the routes on the map and following the text as it leapt forward from one town to the next on the vacant eastern plains or paused for a moment to detail some scene of particular natural beauty in the Rockies.

My first impressions of Montana, then, were fashioned from symbolic representations, the abstractions of sentences and diagrams, from the lines of words on a page and those of highways on a map. Between those lines lay immense, blank middle spaces open to imagination.

On a wall at the ranch hangs a large relief map of southwest Montana, a three-foot by four-foot sheet of plastic film vacuum-molded to recess and smooth the valleys, elevate the high ground, crease and rumple the mountainsides; towns, rivers, and roads are printed in colored ink. Representing about twenty-eight thousand square miles of territory, it exchanges precision of detail for a more comprehensive sense of topographical sculpture that you cannot appreciate from ground level. Like optical instruments, maps alter the scale to reveal what can't be seen by the unaided eye. The making of maps preceded written language by millennia, and cartography is perhaps the first form of recorded storytelling. This three-dimensional miniature at the ranch narrates the logic of a landscape, a dialectic of land and water synthesized in riversheds. It is revealing to read a river on a map in the same way that you'd fish it, moving upstream, following the fractal subdivisions of its network as they climb higher, splitting and resplitting into the most remote clefts of the slopes until they reach the peak of the drainage divide. Trace the perimeter of this uppermost limit, and the notion of a catchment basin needs no other elaboration. Although the size and extent of a watershed always surprises me, more striking still is the perception of its finiteness, so different from the experience of endless flow when you are knee-deep and fishing.

Beyond their obvious utility, maps hold an intrinsic fascination—in their X-ray-like exposure of the anatomy of spaces, in the mesmerizing sense of elevation that feels like a form of flying—and they figure routinely into life at the ranch. We bring an assortment of them with us each summer: ordinary road maps and atlases, topographical maps of the entire state and of adjacent ones, hiking maps, canoeing maps, fishing maps, maps keyed to public and private land ownership, maps of Yellowstone Park, and individual maps of at least half a dozen different rivers. These stay on the dining room table along with the towering stacks of field guides that collapse once or twice daily into a jumbled heap. But they belong together, for a map is really a sort of field guide, and field guides, in the way of all reference books, are really just another form of map. We consult our maps regularly, sometimes surveying well-known territory to answer questions or gain a fresh perspective on the familiar, and sometimes to conduct preliminary reconnaissance of places that seem worth a closer look, frequently for reasons related to fishing. The ranch is fortunately situated in this respect. Within a driving radius of ninety minutes or so lies enough trout water to keep an industrious angler busy for a lifetime, and while all roads most certainly do not lead to the ranch, the only one that leads out will take you everywhere else. So sometimes we go, not just in the usual daily detachments of twos and threes but the whole lot of us, striking out for some place we found first on a map.

These outings are particularly favored, and usually instigated, by the nonangling contingent—primarily the Writer, the Intended, and the Hindu—which, though small, is highly influential. Organizing these excursions and getting them on the road can be something of a production, since mornings at the ranch unfold in leisurely, idiosyncratic rhythms that do not lend themselves easily to orchestration. Normally, I rise first, at or before dawn, and watch the sky lighten and listen to the early-morning, rusty-pump screeches of the great horned owls that hunt from the cottonwoods. The Cook arrives before long, and we may spend an hour talking at the kitchen table before the Painter sits down to join us. A while later, the Mechanic shows up, barefoot and disheveled, his mind on pancakes. Bacon and eggs, fruit and pastries appear. The others wander in at intervals, the Writer always last, sometimes materializing just long enough to stoke up a latte, her wholly nonnegotiable preliminary to the day. To suggest forgoing the espresso pot in the interests of time or, conversely, to cast a covetous eye on its contents is to court serious personal harm.

The newly arrived take seats at the small table as they are vacated by the early risers, who then prop themselves against counter edges and doorways. The kitchen gradually fills with half-awake bodies maneuvering about to the refrigerator or toaster, or here or there, the movements of one in the crowded room initiating a lazy chain reaction among the others, who step back or edge sideways to clear a space at the sink or stove or let someone squeeze past. We mill about, caroming softly off the cabinetry, the wallpaper, one another, like slow-moving molecules with coffee cups in random Brownian motion. Because everyone wishes to accommodate the others, no one presumes to fix a specific departure time for the day's junket or to take charge and harness the entropic forces of the morning into usable work that will get us out the door. The Mechanic will sometimes step up on these occasions, surprisingly for a man who puts a premium on his solitude and will disappear for many hours off somewhere by himself. Even so, he keeps a deceptively careful watch on the communal welfare, and beyond that, his admiration for smoothly functioning, well-coordinated mechanisms extends to social ones as well. Helping to launch one of these outings successfully, I suspect, yields the same satisfactions as laying a hardwood floor or rebuilding an engine.

These trips typically involve a trout stream, partly as a concession made to those who fish by those who don't, though mostly because everyone would rather spend the day around water than anywhere else. You wouldn't, however, call them fishing trips in the usual meaning of that term. Whatever angling gets done leans to the casual sort, the type that a serious angler would describe as "taking a few casts," with the understanding that this should not be construed literally but merely in contrast to spending several uninterrupted hours fishing. Nor are these normally long trips. What they lack in distance and duration, however, they more than recover in complexity. Six or eight of us may take part, and as a rule of thumb in such situations, once a group exceeds two people, each additional participant roughly doubles the preparation time and confusion. It's a little like the reproductive dynamics of certain small animals.

Some earnest thinking goes into the matter of food, for while differences of opinion may arise on minor points, we stand unanimously in favor of lunch. The Cook and the Bodhi mastermind the coolers. Others of us round up camp chairs and a roll-up table to hold books, paints, and food when the time arrives. The Writer, the Intended, and the Painter crate up a selection of field guides and collect binoculars. Despite the incidental nature of the fishing, each angler usually brings a full quota of gear, just in case we arrive to find acres of trout rising to a hatch that needs matching, which has so far never once happened. Several of the group load up day packs—with what, I am not sure. Heavy stuff mostly. There are hiking boots for some, rain gear for all, and much scuttling back and forth between the house and cars to assemble the assorted extras that address the needs, comforts, and diversions of everyone. All of this gets heaped, Joad-like, into a couple of rigs, and the whole affair lumbers more or less forward with deep inefficiencies, fantastic redundancies of effort, and strong Chaplinesque overtones. By the scheduled departure time, or an hour or two afterward as the case may be, a general enthusiasm prevails, and we leave the ranch in a two-car caravan with a glad-hearted and slightly reckless sense of adventurousness, J. Thaddeus Toad leading Mr. Magoo off for an airing in the country.

1

PERHAPS ONCE A SEASON OR SO, OUR DESTINATION IS A TRAIL THAT FOLLOWS one of the tributaries of the Madison, a small stream that heads in the peaks at 9,000 feet and descends through a steep, angular crease in the mountainside. This creek mystified me at first, when I was new to the West and unacquainted with the abnormalities of running water in arid country. Where the map alleged this tributary to pass beneath a bridge, I found nothing but a bed of bleached and powdery rock and dismissed it as a seasonal snowmelt channel that dried up in summer. I wouldn't learn for another couple of years that the stream, like so many in the West, had been plumbed with ditches higher up that diverted every last dribble of water for irrigation. Having only fished before in the Midwest and the East, I assumed an inflexible relationship between altitude and running water: the more of the one, the less of the other, just as God or whomever intended. If there was no water down below, there'd be less than none above. But here, a few miles up the parched channel, the trail intercepts the creek above a dam and brings you to a full-blown, thriving trout stream that never completes its downhill run, that exists in strange isolation on a mountain flank, with the trout, I presume, entirely unaware of their bizarre predicament.

The trail begins on rolling rangeland, just below the edge of a forest that cloaks the mountain, and from there climbs into the trees. While I will walk long distances to fish, I have never really grasped the appeal of hiking for its own sake, winding your way among the constantly unfolding glories of nature while staring down at your feet, trying to avoid the loose rock, bulging root, or simple misstep that could plunge you to ruin. The Writer, however, has an astonishing appetite for it, and as the rest of us don sensible shoes and shoulder day packs, she's already geared up and anxious to get moving, possibly owing to a few tankards of espresso at breakfast. Her uniform never varies: overscaled straw visor and its rattlesnake pin, broken-down hiking boots, walking staff, and a waist pack, to which she sometimes affixes a bear bell. This bell has been the object of endless derision over the years. Aside from the questionable efficacy of an ounce of brass in warding off the attentions of a thousand-pound omnivore, it makes a racket, which is of course the point. The Cook finds it especially unendurable, or so he claims publicly, perhaps out of sympathy for the rest of us. Privately, I suspect, he finds some small comfort in it, as he shares my own misgivings about bear country. Grizzlies have in fact been spotted in this watershed at least a couple of times that I know of over the years, though never by us, which the Writer naturally attributes to the bell. It does, however, prove useful in keeping track of the Writer, who will sometimes wander off, helpless against her own indiscriminate curiosity.

At the outset of the trek, she assumes the lead, the rest of us strung along behind her on the path. As mountain trails will, this one parallels the creek, though at most points from a distance of ten or twenty yards, so that the stream shows itself only sporadically through an intervening screen of trees. What water you can see looks fishable, though would not be my first choice for fishing. It cascades steeply around tumbled boulders and shattered rock, a classic high-gradient freestone, turbulent and frothy, descending irregularly in small stair-step pools and bottlenecking through chutes, a confusion of swift and conflicting currents. Much of it flows between steep banks cluttered with jackstrawed deadfalls and brush, nearly enclosed by a low ceiling of undergrowth that leaves little room for the conventional exercise of a fly rod. Positioning yourself to fish a spot can be an ordeal, and the improvised, off-balance casting in close quarters requires the acrobatic contortions of East Indian lovemaking. The water itself, however, is quite pretty.

The trail up this narrow ravine leads alternately into cool, leafy shade and out again into spotlights of heat where the canopy opens up. Patches of wildflowers colonize these sunny spots and draw butterflies—cabbage whites and alfalfa butterflies, delicate blues and extravagant swallowtails patterned like wildcats, checkerspots and commas, fritillaries and tortoise shells—never in great swarms, just singles or pairs, luminous flickers that bounce along on cushions of air rising from the sun-warmed trail. Like mayflies, they seem barely in command of their oversized wings, erratic, uncertain, at the mercy of things. And like mayflies, they are in fact deceptively well-controlled fliers, adept at remaining just beyond your reach even as they appear wholly oblivious to your presence. When the bell stops clanking for a moment, I know the Writer is stalking one for a closer look.

At some point along the way, perhaps during one of the Writer's many moments of distraction, the Mechanic will move to the front of our straggling column, partly I suppose to escape the bell. He does, however, appear a bit more cautious about assuming the lead since the day a few years back when he was nearly broadsided by an adult mountain goat that, for reasons known only to itself, came boring down the mountainside at flank speed and crossed the trail a few feet in front of him. The Cook speculated that it was being chased by a grizzly. But even as that near miss has made the Mechanic a little more hesitant to head the pack, like the Writer he is ultimately powerless against his own nature. Our little machine grinds its way uphill, and he directs its movement and maintains the equipment, keeping an eye on the moving parts for signs of wear, fatigue, or malfunction.

Although not arduous, the trail climbs steeply enough to produce a distinct sense of ascent, of progressively distancing yourself from the low ground, advancing deeper into the timber and higher up the mountain. Inclinations to the vertical surround you—the peaks overhead, the pitch of the trail and stream, the tree trunks that give the illusion of leaning upslope. Everything seems drawn upward. Even the mountains themselves are rising, mostly in imperceptible increments but from time to time in dramatic events. Half a century ago, slippage along the Red Canyon fault, not many miles from here, produced an earthquake of magnitude 7.1 that brought down a mountainside and impounded Quake Lake. The valley floor sank, the peaks rose, and in less than thirty minutes, the vertical distance between them increased by nearly fifteen feet. The geological record chronicles other such violent episodes, and the uplift of the Madison Range still continues, as it has for the past two million years, when the Madison River first began flowing.

After an hour and a half or so, the trail levels out and draws close alongside the stream. The trees pull back a little to create a narrow strip of open land. Too small and shaded to be called a meadow, it's just a flattish spot in the mountains less than a hundred yards long. Here, we choose a comfortable spot by the water, shrug off our packs, and settle in for the day. Field guides and binoculars appear. The Writer goes off to look for secrets. The bell gets a rest. The Painter wanders about, hunting up plants to identify or present to the rest of us, along with commentary on their medicinal roles in folklore and history, which has become a specialty of hers. Others turn their thoughts to trout or flake out on the ground to rest.

Because the terrain drops gently over this stretch of ground, the stream fishes fairly easily, at least compared to the turbulent pockets lower down. It does, however, require some recalibration after a week or two of long casts and leisurely drifts of the fly on the bigger water in the valley. A more exacting occupation up here, fishing calls for accurate deliveries on a short, well-controlled line. Two or three quick feet of drift may be as good as you'll get before the fly drags, and you must pop it out again into another spot the size of a coffee saucer. But like so many little freestone streams, this one often compensates by containing trout that sometimes strike virtually anything you toss their way with such an eager innocence that you feel embarrassed for them. Yet other times, they respond only to exactly the right pattern presented in precisely the right way. You find yourself pulling advanced moves with your fussiest flies of last resort on trout so small they have no conceivable right to your best work, especially on this kind of nutrient-poor, beggars-can't-be-choosers water. It is almost easier to accept the days when the fish don't hit at all; those seem somehow more explicable.

No one cares to pack in the weight of waders and boots, and we bring only a single pair of felt-soled wading sandals to share, which poses no great hardship to anyone since we take along only one rod anyway. Moreover, only a few weeks and a couple of degrees ago, the stream water was snow, and it's still so cold that you can wet-wade it only for ten minutes or so before stumping numbly to shore and rubbing some sensation back into your legs and feet. By this time someone else has usually warmed up enough to take over. We alternate in this fashion, the fishing a form of group entertainment, and the overall atmosphere strongly recalls the evenings spent fishing at the bridge, though without the Hun.

To my knowledge, only rainbows inhabit this water, and though you might reasonably expect to find brown trout on a stream that communicates with the Madison, we have never caught one. The complete absence of water in the lower channel when the browns spawn during the fall could have something to do with this. Cutthroats originally lived here, but I have never seen one or any evidence of one, such as a hybridized fish. The rainbows that have since come to occupy it are exceptionally handsome in their conformation and color, with unusual turquoise vermiculations nearly the same color as the blue halos on a brook trout. I can't say if this color or patterning is unique among rainbows, only that I've never seen it on the species anywhere else. A few times in an angling life, you may run across fish like this, locally particular and so distinctive in some way that you believe you could readily pick one out of a lineup. Perhaps I'm wrong about this, and it owes to faulty memory or not fishing widely enough. But it doesn't diminish the striking beauty of these rainbows, and were you to reproduce them on a canvas, you would choose the palette of a bright afternoon in early fall, flecks of an aqua sky glimpsed through a canopy of forest green streaked with the first reds and golds of changing leaves.

We catch a few trout in places we know well and a few more from well-known places we've never before fished. An angler first works the water by analogy, attending to the echoes of past places, and few types of water better reward this kind of listening than small streams in the mountains. Wherever you find them, they are nearly identical; it is one of their most dependable and charming attributes. The flora and fauna around them may change with geography, but the patterns of current and obstruction, the path water takes over ledge rock and around boulders, the places the trout live are all universal. Even a stream you have never seen before is instantly familiar, and a day spent exploring such water has a quality less of discovery than of recollection. Hiking along this stream brings to mind others, miles and years away. I used to visit a little creek in the Alleghenies with the same faintly peach-colored tint to the tumbling water. For a few weeks each season, the place was enveloped in a veil of yellow swallowtails, thousands of them swirling about like maple leaves in a fall breeze. Two hundred miles farther south, on a mountain tributary very like this one, I found a butterfly I'd never seen before—a Diana fritillary, not technically rare but unusual for the area, so large and distinctive it could not be misidentified. I was with the Painter on a morning in the years before we were married. There have been dozens of other streams, many of them in the East, and most of those fished in the company of the Bodhi or the Cook or the Painter over half a lifetime ago. And as we walk along the bank now, trading off the rod at each new spot, it seems impossible to me that so much time could have passed.

We spend the middle hours of the day this way, with some fishing and much talk that circles back to summers gone by, a turn of conversation perhaps suggested by the gain in altitude and the prospect it affords of what lies behind and far off. Time behaves differently at higher elevations. It runs both more quickly and more slowly than it does below, and the season here appears to rush ahead even as it lags behind. The long cold of a mountain winter condenses the summer into a few short weeks. You can see it in the underbrush and the trees. We think of winter as a season of dormancy after half a year of sprouting, leafing, flowering, and fruiting. But up high, the year consists mostly of dormancy, its season of growth the exception rather than the rule. The warm weeks of summer bring with them a concentrated intensity as plants must grow, bloom, and set seed all in less time than it takes to ripen a green apple down below.

Up here, wildflowers long gone from the valley bloom the landscape back to early summer even as the compressions of altitude force other, opposing changes—a barely perceptible fading of color in leaves and the first suggestion of curling and desiccation at the tips, foretelling the exhaustion that succeeds extravagance. The far end of summer, never far off, is already brought closer as a dry smell on the air and a quality in the light. The sun arcs across a thin slice of sky above the canyon and sets prematurely below the horizon of the ridgeline, persuading you that the day is more advanced than it really is, like afternoons in autumn. In the foreshortening of summer, you can sense the urgency in a landscape where beginnings and endings are equally present, can feel more sharply the passing of time and time having already passed. Hovering at the edges of the day is an intimation of that nonspecific longing that arrives with fall. Like the high country, fall exists as both a place and a promontory. You can see a long way from autumn.

Then someone says we should probably go. We round up our stuff and strap on packs and start down. Back at the trailhead, there is beer on ice and a return to the heart of deep summer.

2

EVERY FEW SEASONS, WE TAKE A DAY AND DRIVE TO THE BIG HOLE RIVER. The road from the ranch crosses a low saddle between the Tobacco Root and Gravelly ranges that divides the Madison Valley from that of the Ruby River, where we fished once in a plague of deerflies that swarmed straight from the pages of Exodus and chewed us up so mercilessly that even now the mere thought of it gives me skin lesions. From the pass, the road drops into Alder Gulch, where, in May 1863, a handful of itinerant prospectors found gold. Naturally, they tried to keep it quiet, but you know how these things go, and almost overnight the place devolved into the kind of asylum typically associated with mineral strikes. Within a year, ten thousand of the simple-hearted and hopeful had arrived with pans and sluice boxes. They established a string of makeshift settlements centered around Virginia City but essentially continuous from Alder to Summit, a long stretch that came to be called "Fourteen-Mile City." Operating under the proven political principle that you don't get fed if you're not at the trough, the territorial government moved from Bannack to Virginia City. Three years after that, the easy gold that could be extracted by hand was mostly gone and the placer boom ended.

It would take until the turn of the century for the truly earnest pillage to begin, when in 1899 the Conrey Placer Mining Company unleashed steam-powered floating dredges to work the deeper gravels. Over the next two decades, they devoured over thirty-seven million cubic yards of river stone from the Alder Creek floodplain and excreted a seven-mile strip of stagnant dredge ponds and tailing piles that remains visible today, over eighty years after the gluttony ended. In a curious turn of events pregnant with a meaning I can't quite deliver, one of the original Conrey investors, upon his death, bequeathed his controlling interest in the company to Harvard University, which tugged at the golden nipple for the next twenty years—yet another little piece of the West devastated to enrich the East. A few decades later, in a gesture to modernity, hard-rock mining threw a little cyanide into the mix.

It is a relief to reach Twin Bridges, which I have always regarded warmly, in large part, I confess, because some outstanding fly rods come from a shop in this small and unpretentious town. From here, we veer off onto one of those shortcuts that probably saves no time but appeals for other reasons. On this gravel road that winds through the hills behind McCartney Mountain, the traveling gets dusty and slow and slower still over the washed-out side-cuts and rutted switchbacks. You see few houses or ranches, only rolling rangeland, and the trip always summons up images of what rural travel in Montana involved in the days of the WPA guide. We pick up the river at Melrose and continue upstream.

Above the town of Wisdom, the Big Hole Valley unfolds in one of the most striking expanses of mountains and bottomland in Montana, sweeping and dramatic yet somehow more humanly scaled than the Madison Valley, though fewer humans in fact live here. Despite its high elevation and rugged containment by the Beaverhead and Pioneer ranges, the gently sloping valley floor has a pastoral quality that one normally associates with less severe places, and in the upper reaches, even the river assumes a bucolic, spring creek–like character. This watershed produced little in the way of precious metals, and the few claims established here never amounted to much. In the last century, wildcatters sank a few exploratory wells for oil and gas and found themselves drilling through over two and a half miles and several million years' worth of accumulated geological fill before striking bedrock. Their efforts didn't come to much either. Extracting a different resource, however, proved simpler and more successful. Plenty of sluices were built here, not the kind made of wood but the type dug into the land, mining not gold but water—a more valuable commodity that has incited more acrimonious and consequential disputes. In years past, we fished the river a few times in the hopes of catching grayling; one of the last remaining fluvial populations lives in the Big Hole. That venture never amounted to much, and the fish continue to decline as dewatering and habitat damage lower the summer water flows and raise the temperature, both to nearly lethal levels. During recent seasons of drought, the official response, in a classic form of non sequitur management, has been to close the fishing in August, which certainly doesn't hurt but goes no distance at all toward solving the actual problem.

On one of our trips here, we set out to fish a tributary of the Big Hole, another small, pocket-water creek in the mountains, though this one requiring no hike to reach. We had, uncharacteristically, a specific purpose: to return to the ranch with dinner. The tributary, we knew from hearsay and the Bodhi's own investigations of a year earlier, held a large number of small brook trout that the bureaucratic descendants of the people who'd stocked them now wanted to be rid of, passively acknowledging that "mistakes had been made" in transplanting this species from the East. The resident rainbows, however, a species no more native to the stream than French fries to France, would remain protected. The nonangler may well puzzle over this policy that sacrifices one nonindigenous trout to the interests of another, pointing out that it makes no real sense. Anglers, however, grasp the logic of it in ways they find difficult to articulate, mainly because trying to do so would expose the essential irrationality behind it. But even confirmed catch-and-release fishermen, and I would count us among them, have no real reservations about this kind of hairsplitting among trout—we do it ourselves all the time—and if a few fish in the creel happen to result from it, so much the better. I recall the daily bag at the time as something like twenty-five brook trout per person per day, a liberal figure to encourage their removal. A single limit would serve us all generously, and we felt confident of getting it. With five reasonably experienced anglers fishing a species of trout not historically known for its circumspection, how hard could it be? The answer, of course, suggests the problem with all rhetorical questions.

We spread out a tenement-like day camp in a stand of lodgepole pine along the creek, and given the small size of the water, we split up and spread out. Some drove a few miles farther on to fish, leaving the nearer stretches to the Cook and me. Rather than leapfrogging spots in the interests of efficiency, we elected to fish together and take turns, as the stream contained no pools or runs large enough for two. We've shared rivers this way countless times in many places, and both of us remarked that the little creek before us quite closely resembled one we'd hiked up decades earlier in the Adirondacks. We were fishing brook trout there as well and covered several miles of water, eventually ending up, as we discovered afterward, deep in the recesses of a private compound owned by the Rockefellers. We did rather well, too, as I remember, though our local friends couldn't figure out why we hadn't been caught. Two years later, the Bodhi and I returned to the same creek and found that acid rain had wiped out nearly every living creature.

After the others had gone, the Cook and I started upstream. For some reason, he seemed determined to give me most of the water and all of the best. When his turn came around, he'd wave me ahead, claiming his leader needed work or his fly needed tending to, which was a lie, or that he had to sit down and ease a stitch in his side, which was true, a mysterious and persistent complaint of his over the past couple of years. I pointed out helpfully that a person of his advanced age (about forty-six at the time) and deteriorating condition might consider orthopedic waders, that a lot of old guys were wearing them these days. He in return delivered an extended and partially accurate litany of my own middle-age infirmities. I brought up his receding hairline and the titanium screws in his knee, a permanent legacy of going full court with guys half as old and twice as good. And so on, back and forth in the kind of exchange that long ago became automatic between us, the white noise of old friends.

Half in earnest, I suggested that his problem might stem from a faulty gallbladder, an apparently optional organ I'd never paid much attention to until a few summers earlier, when the Painter required an emergency trip to Bozeman, where she ultimately parted with hers. The daughter of a doctor, she has always mistrusted physicians, but the problem had gotten severely out of hand and demanded immediate measures. Minor complications arose afterward, and we spent an extra day in the hospital taking slow, recuperative walks through the corridors, she dragging an IV stand behind her, a polished chromium cyborg with blinking LED eyes and outstretched arms proffering on-demand morphine. Standing at a large window looking out over the Bridger Mountains, she said, "I haven't felt this good in years." I wagered not. The Cook, however, insisted that his own gallbladder was in top form and could kick my gallbladder's ass in a fair fight anytime, and then fished the rest of the day to prove it.

We saw no sign of trout for better than an hour, content to surrender ourselves to all the persuasions of a mountain creek that convince you upstream just to look at the next spot ahead, the next proposition it advances from the first premises of water and stone. Arriving at one pool, we stepped over that inexplicable dividing line you sometimes cross, above which trout suddenly appear. All at once we got into fish, one or two from the plausible spots and more from the better places, all of them rainbows, but not a one with turquoise markings. Most of them went about six inches long, though we caught our share of small ones, too, and they rose without guile to whatever we showed them. At first, we wondered idly when we'd start running into brook trout. Probably higher up, we thought, but with time and patience in our favor we found little need to rush or worry.

When the rainbows kept coming, and the hours kept going, the interests of efficiency we'd earlier dismissed acquired a new and pressing relevance. We fished in the growing consciousness that, as far as creeling dinner, we weren't exactly holding up our end or any fraction of it. And should things continue in this vein, the others of our party, the Mechanic in particular, would take the opportunity for a good-natured but persistent abuse of the type that the Cook and I, in the spirit of Christian selflessness, have always believed it is better to give than receive. We set to our work with a new determination, knowing that should we strike just a couple of good pools and tap even a small lode of brook trout, our fortunes would be made. Not yet desperate, but getting there, we sluiced the shallows with dry flies and dredged the deeper places with beadhead droppers, sorting through the inconsequential rainbows for the gleam of brook trout. We split up and worked separate claims, which had the predictable effect of doubling the number of rainbows we caught. A small stream does not present a large number of options. You can't, for instance, fish a different type of water where you think the brookies might hold; all the trout there are will be in the only water there is. We made radical changes in fly style, taking only more rainbows, until at last I slapped a hamster and caught nothing. Skipping a long section of water and hiking upstream was our last remaining option, but the only perceptible result was that the rainbows averaged a little smaller.

A moment will sometimes arrive in fishing, infrequently but unfortunately, when you can see the day taking a turn, heading south, going sour in ways that you neither anticipated nor seem capable of stopping. Any number of incidental circumstances might precipitate the decline—bad luck, bad weather, bad water, bad company, or just you fishing badly—but in time it expands to become a free-floating and generalized pall of frustration or discouragement or ill humor that descends over everything. Nearly always, however, you can trace it to the same cause: you've invested too much in too little. It isn't necessarily a question of unrealistically high expectations, of wanting too much; but in a way it's the opposite, a matter of contracted expectations, of wanting too specifically. It is the same impulse that causes some people to marry badly. Define the terms of success too exclusively and you hang the weight of your satisfaction on a hook too insubstantial to hold it. For reasons that had ceased to do with a cast-iron skillet, I wanted brook trout, and to stake one's well-being on catching fish is invariably a fool's wager. Perhaps other anglers had gotten to the brook trout before me and cleaned the place out; perhaps I resented their cupidity sating itself ahead of mine. But a dark cloud had moved in over the afternoon, and I fished under it in deteriorating spirits and a gloom of my own making. Every perfect little rainbow came as a letdown and was released as an irritation. They might as well have been chubs.

If the Cook sensed anything amiss, he took it philosophically and fished on, untroubled, like a man who knew precisely where he stood: alongside lovely water on a picturesque mountain stream and, as if that weren't enough, catching trout. When he called down from the next pool in a small chain of cascades, I looked up, thinking maybe our moment had finally come, but he tapped an imaginary wristwatch with his index finger and motioned me up. We broke down our rods, headed cross-country through the lodgepoles out to the road, and walked back to camp. The others, who'd already returned, told pretty much the same story, not a whiff of brook trout anywhere, and then talked on about all the fine water and rainbows they'd seen. Though by every meaningful measure, as I would appreciate in retrospect, it had been a good day and in ways an exceptional one, I felt mainly a disappointment absurdly out of proportion to its object. Arriving in new territory with a desire to extract and possess has always had a way of changing things through misaligned priorities and a skewed sense of wealth.

Driving back, we passed again the ulcerated miles of century-old dredge spoils along Alder Gulch that, in two decades, had netted less than ten million dollars' worth of gold, a few drops that had dissolved quickly and long ago into the national cash flow, as though they'd never even existed.

On our way to the ranch, the Cook suggested that we swing by the butcher shop in Ennis and pick up something for a late dinner.

3

EVERY NOW AND AGAIN, USUALLY FOR THE BENEFIT OF FRIENDS WHO HAVE not seen it before, we drive to Yellowstone Park, though not without stopping first in the town of West Yellowstone, where the Writer might secure a couple of latte grandes to go, without which she would evidently meet some piteous end. The park makes for one of those excursions where you very much hope, the popular maxim notwithstanding, that getting there will be significantly less than half the fun. The congestion in high season drags traffic to a claustrophobic standstill. You must imagine yourself at a dead halt on the roadway in 95-degree heat, walled in on three sides by multistory tour buses disgorging carbon monoxide into your small and rapidly diminishing pocket of oxygen in order to get some small feeling for the grandeur that is Yellowstone in August. But you are there too, like everyone else, which leaves little legitimate room for complaint.

The landscape itself, of course, ranks among the most fascinating and sublime anywhere, particularly in the caldera, which though not alive in the technical sense, behaves like a living thing. The geological record indicates that massive volcanic eruptions have taken place there about once every 600,000 years, the lava flows oozing all the way to California, which is a consoling thought to some. That the most recent event occurred 620,000 years ago makes one look back on Cold War notions of "the big one" with something akin to nostalgia. The tourists at ground zero should at least have a spectacular if brief display, while many millions of the rest of us will just suffocate in a visually unremarkable poisonous cloud.

We generally tour the usual sights, but when escorting visiting anglers, we may head to Buffalo Ford on the Yellowstone River, though rarely with much eagerness. Because it numbers among the best-known, most convenient, and most popular access points in the Park, I always feel not so much like a tourist, which I am and have accepted, but like an angler with no imagination or initiative. Invariably, you find the water crowded. The trout, already caught several times each by August, betray symptoms of existential ennui and when hooked swim slowly to your feet and roll onto their sides so that you may remove the fly. The whole scene on and around the river radiates the barely suppressed subcurrent of weirdness that always suffuses tourist destinations. But it's also one of those places that every angler, if only for the sake of credentials, should fish at least once. And so we sometimes take a trip to the ford, both in the conventional sense of traveling there and in the more colloquial, Grateful Dead understanding of the term. It is always an occasion of the mildly strange.

A group of us arrived one August morning not many years ago, and finding the immediate water completely occupied by what appeared to be some sort of rug beaters' convention, the Bodhi and I struck off downstream, passing a number of other anglers with the same idea, until we finally came upon an open spot to fish. It proved to be one of those "looking glass" holes—not really a pool, just a deep bowl in the river with a flow so uniform that the surface of the water was almost perfectly smooth. Every detail right down to the bottom stood out vividly, including eight or ten nice cutthroats finning along a seam formed by a chunk of stone the size of a refrigerator. We could see the white interiors of their mouths as the trout opened them to feed. The fish held five or six feet down in a squirrelly current break; getting a fly precisely in the right drift line entailed some trial and error and luck, but when it all came together, the trout took without the slightest reservation.

The Bodhi, as I remember, hooked the first one, and as he wrestled it to the surface, the commotion drew the attentions of a pelican that must have concealed itself nearby. It immediately took after the fish, as pelicans will, and though they are already by nature quite good at it, this one had clearly worked out an advanced system involving visiting anglers. The pelican took a swipe at the trout, which instantly shot downriver to a tongue of fast water and pulled free. This probably happens all the time, but we'd never seen it before. With some hand clapping and hopping about and menacing gestures, we drove the bird off. But when I hooked the second fish, it returned and, having apparently drawn useful conclusions from its first attempt, had the situation well under control this time. The trout wasn't going to stand a chance, so I took a wrap of fly line around my hand and gave it a yank to break off the fish. The pelican swam to the far bank and waited.

As we contemplated our next move, a park ranger came walking down the trail, a woman in an immaculately pressed shirt, slacks with a straight-razor crease, and the stern hat of her profession. She wore a thick leather belt that surrounded her with ominous black snap-closing compartments bulging with the mysteries of law enforcement. I react to uniformed authority of any sort with a kind of involuntary unraveling, a reflex that dates back to the cassocks and habits of my parochial-school upbringing. An accelerating nervousness overwhelms me. Anxious to demonstrate that I am, for the most part, an everyday law-abiding citizen, I talk a little too much and a little too fast and compulsively begin to account for my recent whereabouts and what business brings me here, paying scrupulous attention to those details that might prove useful in exonerating me from any conceivable wrongdoing, giving every indication that, except for a few things that couldn't possibly be relevant to our present situation, I have nothing to hide, and generally carrying on in much the way I have always imagined guilty people behave, even though I haven't been accused of anything. This performance goes beyond the attempt to argue my blamelessness of any specific infraction and seeks to establish in advance a larger, more universal innocence of everything. Naturally, as a result, I attract suspicion.

The Bodhi, who suffers no such dismantlings, struck up a conversation with her, which I joined when it became evident that I wouldn't be serving any time. I briefly considered seeking her advice on the pelican matter, but thinking back on it now, what with the ice scraper and all, I'm thankful that some instinct warned me away from submitting the problem to a park official. In the course of talking with her, we asked if she patrolled this section of water every day. "No," she answered, a little wearily, "I'm following that," and pointed to the river. It took a few seconds, but we finally spotted it: a dead buffalo. A massive beast to begin with, it had grown bloated and buoyant with some unspeakable gas, bobbing on the chop in a lazy, stiff-legged spin, glancing off rocks and snags with the gentle, slow-motion rebounds of a beach ball. It drifted along in a manner both comical and oddly touching, in the way that any wild animal in reduced circumstances—say, a chimpanzee dressed in a basketball uniform—always moves one to a kind of sadness. She went on to explain that she was tracking the carcass to make sure it didn't lodge on a shoal or hang up in a deadfall somewhere along the bank where its decomposing wretchedness might attract a grizzly. She didn't appear to relish the work. Her tone of voice betrayed a hint of fatigue and beneath that, it seemed to me, a touch of indignation or resentment, as though maybe she thought she'd been singled out for this chore because she happened to be a woman. Possibly she had. I thought that spending a day pursuing this novelty downriver sounded like it might be fun, but then I've never done it. Maybe it gets old or you run into a lot of bears.

The buffalo glided silently past us, and she trudged after it. The Bodhi and I discussed the prospect of gathering up the others and driving to the Lower Falls. Watching seventeen hundred pounds of putrefying buffalo in a 308-foot vertical free fall is not an opportunity that comes your way every day; maybe once in a lifetime, if you're lucky. But the Bodhi, who has always been quick at such things, ballparked a calculation and estimated that the timing would be close, depending on traffic. So we went back to trying to fish and not feed the pelican at the same time.

Buffalo Ford was the first water we ever fished in the park, the Painter, the Bodhi, and I, along with a couple of friends, one of them the person who would later lead me on so many misconceived quests for secret water.

But he also led us to the Madison Valley for the first time. We drove there from Buffalo Ford and camped on the river for two days, fishing with a lack of results that I find unbelievable now. The most distinct recollection I have preserved from that trip, however, was watching a Fish and Wildlife boat across the river. It was being walked slowly down the far bank by someone in waders holding the stern. The deck was piled with electrofishing equipment, and a second person was handling the electrode while a third netted and measured stunned fish—enormous fish to my eyes, and great numbers of them. The boat was almost two hundred feet away, so I didn't get a very clear look, but every so often I caught the amber flash of a big brown trout turned broadside in the net. I followed them down for a hundred yards or so, speechless at the number of fish they turned up from just a narrow swath of water along the bank.

Not until a few years later, when I started fishing the river regularly, many times along that same shoreline, did I realize that most of what they'd netted were whitefish. But that scene continued to figure powerfully in my imagination of Montana even after I knew.

About two years after I'd finished learning nothing about the writers of the Great Depression and had shelved the WPA guides, I found myself tracing a route on a different map of Montana, a road atlas, as the Painter and I, having married a week earlier, packed our worldly traps into the back of an eighteen-foot rental truck, hitched an aging Datsun to the rear bumper, and on a morning in early August set off from the East Coast to the Pacific Northwest. We made the Black Hills around the middle of the fourth day out, where the Painter took over to drive. I'd been behind the wheel twenty of the previous twenty-eight hours and needed to shut my eyes.

Having never driven this truck or any other, she was already apprehensive and made more so by the questionable commitment of the car in tow to the trailer hitch—an on-again, off-again relationship that had inconvenienced us several times since we'd started out. But she gamely agreed to spell me. As I collapsed into sleep on the passenger's side, she was hunched over the wheel, staring grimly ahead, and white-knuckling down the interstate at forty miles per hour, our progress steady but of the careful sort. I regained consciousness a few hours later to find her, elbow propped on the open window, the rush of warm afternoon air whisking away the smoke from a cigarette, steering with two fingers, spellbound by the expanses of a wheat-colored West receding away to the curve of the earth under an immense sapphire sky. We were dispensing with the last of Wyoming, and leaning over for a peek at the dashboard, I could see the line on the speedometer marked "80." The needle was nowhere in sight, and I decided not to lean farther. "This is actually kind of fun," she said. "You know, I've always liked driving."

In this spirit we entered Montana on what the WPA guidebook had identified as U.S. Highway 10 but was now I-90, not quite flying but driving at a low altitude through the rolling hills of Little Bighorn country, our rate of travel undiminished. We blew into Bozeman just after dusk. It was a mild and uncommonly beautiful August evening, the skies clear and the air balmy with what I've since come to recognize as the first hint of September in it. The last of the setting sun lit the peaks of the Bridger Mountains with a warm, copper radiance and cast the valley into hazy, blue-gray shadows. Even in town, the breeze carried that dry, dusty, hay smell of late-summer range. Neither of us had ever been to Montana before, nor had we anticipated the elation that slowly mounted as we watched the landscape in the waning light.

On the bed in a motel room, we opened the map again to take a closer look at our position and get our bearings. I didn't know it then, but we were, as the crow flies, less than fifty miles from the ranch, at just that time of the summer that would become so familiar to us in the years that followed. The Painter examined the atlas intently. Although we were headed to Oregon the next day, she looked up and said, "Maybe we should just stay here instead," knowing it wasn't possible. Looking back now, I think that her remark, as she held the map in her hand, may have contained the first words of a narrative that, a few years down the road, we would begin to invent. For a story is a map of sorts, plotted with the coordinates of life, though not necessarily to scale.

12

Wading for Godot

VLADIMIR: One is what one is.

ESTRAGON: No use wriggling.

VLADIMIR: The essential doesn't change.

—Samuel Beckett

Much of the technical fly-fishing literature at which anglers have suckled for over a century possesses acutely hallucinogenic properties. Ingesting it produces weird distortions, and never more so than in the matter of hatching insects and rising fish, which generations of recreational users have been induced to believe are the default condition of the average trout stream and a routine component of the ordinary angler's experience in fishing. While never nakedly advanced, this gravity-defying assumption hovers so invisibly in the background that it verges on a form of corruption. In these instructional texts, for which so many trees have given their beautiful lives, the expert always arrives streamside to meet with hatching flies and feeding trout as though by appointment. From the platform of this manufactured fantasy, he launches directly into the technical counsel: first you determine which insects are hatching, then which ones the trout are rising to, then which stage of the life cycle the fish appear to favor, and so on. The immediate effect is much like reading an instructional book on poker in which the first chapter unhelpfully details the betting strategies when you're dealt a full house.

The cumulative consequences of long-term exposure are more damaging. The angler who regularly steps into a river at the recommended hour and sees neither a single insect nor a solitary rise feels not so much disappointed as personally inadequate, like a man who finds himself incapable of appreciating French cinema. The experts, he feels, would not have this problem. Something in the system has let him down. He pities his small patch of water, then discreetly sniffs himself and smells failure. Consulting his watch, he weighs the thought of packing up and heading back, perhaps in time to shoot the front nine or touch up the hedge clippers and lay waste to the shrubbery. But in the end, he sits on the riverbank and waits.

As a general principle, hanging around in hopes that fate will deliver the goods is not a paying proposition. To pass one's days fixed on the future, expectantly or otherwise, waiting for something—a lucky break or the latest lab results, a gold watch and a certificate, a miracle or the other shoe to drop—is, in the larger scheme, the drama of existence deferred, the tragedy of the unlived life. But in angling, it is commonplace, and in fishing hatches, virtually assured. The arrival of insects operates much like annual precipitation: over time, it generally plays out according to estimates, but you have no guarantee of just what the weather will be like on any given day. Nothing bespeaks both hope and the perils of optimism more than the thought of rising trout. And if you wish to fish the hatch, you will almost certainly spend time in the passive voice and conditional mood—might, should, would, could have been—awaiting what may or may not occur.

Which accounts for how I happen to be on a short piece of that long transitional stretch of the Madison where the character of the river gradually changes from the pocket water above to the islands and channels below. The current here proceeds at the pace of a purposeful walk, the lightly riffled expanse of its broad middle split here and there into chevrons of calm behind boulders or broken to a coarse chop by midriver shoals. It presents handsome, trouty water everywhere, but nowhere more than at its edge, where the riverbed spreads an apron of boulders, some partially submerged, others entirely so, in a narrow band along the bank. Variously shaped and sized, pushed into random placement over millennia by surge after surge of spring runoff and jostled about by seismic tremors, these stones produce one of the elegant, accidental arrangements of forms that appear everywhere in this landscape, in the groves of cottonwood, the fretted skyline of peaks, the meandering rim of the benches. Skeins of current spool out between boulders and unravel among the stones, the furrowed strands dividing and plaiting together again with the serene precision of a Zen rock garden. Sitting at the water's edge on an ottoman-sized block of schist flecked with pink and black and worn with an accommodating butt-shaped depression, I study this prospect and think that it could be no other way, that any small change would alter the whole and leave it not half so beautiful.

Behind me the valley floor spreads eastward, inclining gently upward for almost a mile. It climbs the flank of a bench, levels out to a short plateau, and then curves up the arc of a pine-covered slope in sweeping, high-drama crescendo to the mountaintop. The low bevel of a late-afternoon sun chisels the landscape into relief, raising textures flattened by the weight of the midday glare, carving shadows in the mountainside draws, behind the swells and folds of rangeland, along the tree lines, in the crisp outline of grasses. In this slant of whiskey-colored light, dimension returns to the land like an animal out of hiding. Across the river, the high ground lies much closer. The wandering edge of the western bench sends a blunt, peninsular thumb toward the river, raising a backdrop that will in a while put the stony margin of the far shore in an indigo shade. That's where the caddisflies will show first, if they show at all—in the shadows along the bank—and I wish I were over there. But with the deceptively powerful current and deep water, only someone with a severe head wound or a death wish would try to cross the river here. And even averting catastrophe, he'd have to get back. In the dark.

The caddis hatch, or the prospect of it, has brought me to this particular spot with, as it turns out, plenty of time to spare. Just how much I estimate in a rough measurement once shown to me, extending an arm to the west and resting the bottom of a clenched fist on the horizon; each fist height's distance to the sun marks an hour until sunset, each finger width fifteen minutes. I am nearly a fist and three fingers early. The caddis will not come, if they come, until the light leaves the water. But in these waning days of August, the window between dusk and too dark to fish is closing down, and should the bugs arrive, you'd hate to miss a minute of it. Still, to be sitting on the bank staring into the late-afternoon glare almost two hours before the earliest possible onset of a hypothetical event isn't strictly required. It's just how I do it, inclined all my life to cheat out the front edges of fishing, looking, I suppose, to expand time and make things last longer by making them start sooner. In this wishful calculus, if you arrive and prepare yourself, if you set the stage, things will commence—the first light of a fishing day, the first sea-run cutthroat of the season, the first caddisfly of the evening. And the inevitable outcome of trying to elongate time like this is that you end up with plenty of it on your hands.

I've waited before in this very spot, on other days in other years, but never so late in the season, which casts additional doubt on an already dubious enterprise. Even with dusk a short while away, the sun still pounds down a ferocious heat, and this bank has no shade. I've already fished much of the day, as I have pretty much for nearly four straight weeks, and am feeling like I look: a little baked, not yet burned out but unmistakably overcooked around the edges. Chest waders are rolled down to the waist, suspenders drooping like tongues in the hot wind. My swollen right foot, freed from the pinch of a too-tight wading boot, cools in the river to soothe a touch of gout, an absurd condition of my adult life that's had me limping since yesterday morning. There are personal grooming issues—a salty stain of dried perspiration around my hatband, white raccoon mask behind sunglasses, a ten-day stubble over windburned cheeks, appalling fingernails. The fishing vest I've already worn beyond its sunset years is much occupied with falling apart, and my shirt ripens in the heat with its own skunky forensics: insect repellent, blue marine bearing grease, sunscreen, silicone fly paste, several smears of something from lunch. I need a laundromat and a haircut but sit here instead, a vaudeville tramp in trash-bag waders "blaming on his boots," as Vladimir says, "the faults of his feet," fortified with duct-tape delusions and a tinfoil hat waiting for news of the Great Unrevealed.

"Perhaps," as Vladimir says, "he's a halfwit."

Perhaps he is. But you will spend some fraction of your fishing in wait, and when gauged against the putative aim—catching something—that fraction is large. In one sense, casting the fly is itself just a preliminary to waiting for a strike, and all the maneuvering into position and fancy presentations and line-mending tricks are but measures undertaken to extend the drift and so prolong the wait. Nonanglers, whose impressions of the sport incline to trolling or the bobber, readily grasp this whole idea; it underlies the widespread notion that fishing requires patience, which here in the Empire of Instant Results automatically renders it boring. But

William James, who had an opinion on practically everything, pragmatic and otherwise, once pointed out that boredom originates in perception and results "from being attentive to the passage of time itself." The angler labors under no such inconvenience and routinely misplaces large chunks of time, entire afternoons, whole days, significant portions of a life, with no idea of where they have gone or any specific recollection of how they disappeared. You can certainly become bored while fishing, but only if you ask too much of it or expect the wrong things.

Not all waiting, however, occupies one in the same way; nor can the distinction between waiting and fishing always be cleanly drawn. Poled soundlessly over the flats in a saltwater skiff, you will quite probably spend a great deal of time on the casting deck, rod in one hand, fly in the other, loops of slack line arranged at your feet, essentially just standing there. But at the same time, you work to maintain a condition of high vigilance and scan the water for streaks of shadow on the bottom, an agitated patch of the surface, the shape of a fish against a background of turtle grass, or a small fleet of bonefish tails that, at a distance, look oddly like a mayfly hatch. In this intensely alert form of inactivity, concentration strenuously searches for an object, a kind of fishing and waiting at the same time. And you might return from such a day, not once putting a fly in the water but wrung out with the exertion of doing, to all appearances, nothing at all, exhausted from the effort of prolonged and unfulfilled readiness.

While not nearly as taxing, keeping vigil before a hatch perhaps represents a purer form of waiting since it is unalloyed with any sense of actively participating in your own destiny. Once you've wagered on a time and place, the matter is pretty much out of your hands. "Nothing to be done," as Estragon says. You don't go to the fish but let them come to you, not really searching, just watching. And only an angler of superhuman discipline does not, in time, succumb to the sedative inducements of moving water, drifting in and out of a pleasantly narcotized inattention, while some autonomic, subcortical awareness stands sentinel and scans the water for rings. Should it glimpse a little anomaly in the pattern of the flow, an inconsistency that just doesn't look right, it'll shake the rest of you awake—*Hey! Was that a rise?*—and you'll instantly return to yourself from wherever you've been and study the surface with lavish attention, elaborately scrutinizing each Talmudic line of current for some sign, some irregularity that might betray the onset of the hatch. They are usually false alarms, the consequences of a well-meaning but overactive hopefulness trying to put things in the best light. And before too long, your concentration disengages itself by degrees, and the water you are watching imperceptibly transforms itself once again into the gently rocking aquarium of your own thoughts.

Still, you might do much while waiting, should you wish to do it, and the trout angler has the advantage of a fishing vest, that large repository of small occupations that surround him in a great fuss. He rarely finds himself at a loss for something to be about. The thermometers, collapsible insect seines, hand lenses, and other appurtenances of the diagnostician offer at least the illusion of purpose, and for a few seasons many years ago I wielded these gizmos in high resolve but could never get them to produce much in the way of vendible results. By temperament, I'm more of a fly-box man anyway. While I've lived long enough to know better, and though the melancholy truth of the converse has been repeatedly demonstrated to me, I nonetheless share the pervasive American faith in pharmaceutical therapies and believe that the various hatch-related maladies that might afflict an angler can be treated with the proper prescription of fly patterns. In this regard, I am a walking drugstore. Three and a half fingers before dusk, I consult my little dispensary and, in advance concession to the various malfunctions I have come to expect, pin to a ribbed foam patch on my shoulder the following: three #16 Deer-Hair Caddis, identical to the one already on my tippet, understanding that I will pull the string on the first fish or two and pop off the fly; three #18 CDC Caddis in the likely event that I have misremembered the size of the insect; three #16 Warren Emergers if the high-riding patterns don't ring up a sale; three #16 Emergent Sparkle Pupa for the same reason; three #14 Beadhead Caddis Pupa should matters come to that; and a pair of bushy #12 Deer Hair Caddis that, if the best comes to pass, I will be able to see in the last flush of failing light. Arranged in two orderly rows, they have the vaguely martial formality of a fresh box of cigars, each obedient conscript awaiting its turn at a hatch that may or may not materialize.

These preparations notwithstanding, the Madison where and when I fish it is not much of a hatch river, though it is pretty fair dry-fly water. The big seasonal productions—the cast-of-thousands Mother's Day caddis, the Busby Berkeley extravaganza of the salmonflies—closed down weeks or months ago. Far upriver, in the first few miles below Quake Lake, you can still find some hatches, even now in late August—mayflies in the first couple of hours of morning and again with caddis in the last couple before dark. Less than legendary in scale, they take place dependably enough to produce angler gridlock for much of the day, a situation aggravated by the laws of man and nature. You cannot legally fish this stretch from a boat, nor do the insects appear uniformly throughout it, both of which contribute to a dispiriting congestion of bank fishermen coming and going, milling about, jockeying for a place in line. My tolerance for this bus-terminal atmosphere has declined steadily. I've been told many times that this section of river holds a disproportionately large number of disproportionately large trout, and while I probably disgrace myself by admitting it, I care little for this water and rarely fish it.

All trout streams are instructive, and a big one teaches big things, foremost among them that a river observes the ways of the larger universe—it bestows its blessings unequally, to all appearances at random, and frequently not at all. On my water, in my seasons, whatever hatches occur are usually small and erratic, fleeting and fickle as a child's whim. From midsummer on, grasshoppers compensate to an extent, though less reliably than one would like, as they depend to some degree on favorable early-summer weather. Even then, they wind up in the water only by chance, a botched hop or a strong breeze, and so good fishing reduces to an extended series of lucky accidents, making grasshoppers less a true hatch than a windfall—evidence that the cosmic zookeeper will toss a pork chop now and then to even his humblest creatures, lo even unto the angler.

But proper hatches, ones that unfold according to the ordinary rules of engagement, appear on my water fitfully and inexplicably, without notice or precedent or sequel and, above all, locally. A brief flurry of caddis may be confined to a short side channel or, as I happened upon one year, pale morning duns emerging in a slick behind a single boulder among dozens strewn along a lengthy stretch of shoreline. Mayflies hatched gleefully on perhaps ten square yards of the surface, while virtually identical real estate up and down the bank for quite some distance remained completely vacant. Moreover, life seems to favor statistical lopsidedness—flat tires happen mostly at night; the telephone always rings just as you step into the shower; a daytime doorbell invariably signals someone peddling salvation—and I'm most likely to come upon one of these freakish hatches just as it's tapering to conclusion rather than ramping up, just in time to see the last few flies vanish in the last few rings and get a taste of what I missed. Over the years, I've shown up for hatches of blue-wing olives, pale morning duns, at least two types of caddis, and a fall of flying ants that the evidence suggests was a Roman holiday for the trout, all just as the curtain was coming down.

It tends to happen like this, except when events unfold at the other perverse extreme. On a warm, bright afternoon, the Cook and I fished a stretch below Ennis, wading among the happy confusion of islands. As commonly occurs on these bluebird days, clouds began massing up on the peaks of the Tobacco Roots, slid down the eastern slope, and rolled out in a low, gray mattress directly overhead. The temperature dropped and a little rain began to fall. Almost instantly, mayflies appeared, at first just a scattering of sails on the surface, then more and more, and as the shower continued, hundreds and hundreds of them everywhere—big ones, flavs we would later determine, the first we'd ever seen. Flies drifted down every riffle and band of bankside current, and we spent the next thirty or forty minutes hurrying from place to place looking for rising fish. When the front passed over, the back side loosed sheets of wind-driven hail. As the vast regatta of mayflies floated helplessly in this meteor shower, the seams, pools, and eddies accumulated with catastrophes of the capsized and dismasted, the rudderless and marooned. Five minutes later, the sun came out, the flavs stopped hatching, and the river grew quiet once more, as though nothing remarkable had occurred.

The whole episode lasted perhaps forty-five minutes, and while admitting the difficulty of spotting rises in the rain, the Cook and I felt confident that, between us, we would have seen something had there been something to see. But neither the thousands of flies that hatched through the storm nor the wreckage of the dead and dying afterward brought up a single trout. Not even a little one, not even during one of the thickest mayfly hatches I have ever seen, not even on water that, beyond question, held fish. Every angler of any experience, of course, can and readily will speak of such oddball incidents. The human imagination gravitates more to the singular than the ordinary, and exchanges among fishermen typically highlight the atypical, in which both fish and fishing abound. I mention the flavs here in this same spirit of paradox, as a representative anomaly, emblematic of both the personality of the Madison where and when I fish, and the character of my experiences with it. For on various occasions over the years, I have waited through promising hatches of tricos, yellow sallies, and *Callibaetis* to their equally troutless conclusions.

Whether the fish are sopping up the last few flies just as I arrive, or whether my timing is perfect and the trout are a no-show, these events occur only infrequently, maybe once or twice a season at best. But however erratic, these misses and near misses predictably spur me to an after-the-fact readiness. I spend the evening tying approved imitations, in quantity, and squeezing them into already overworked fly boxes, crushing the patterns beneath and with them the hopes of former hatches that they once signified. The next day, or the next time that similar water and weather conditions prevail, I return to the same place at the same hour, stake out the same water, take care to duplicate as nearly as possible the original set of circumstances, and settle into waiting for an event that has never once repeated itself. The boxes in my vest record these occasions in strata of abandoned flies, a personal Troy of rear-guard actions undertaken against irreproducible events. If nothing else—and there is mostly nothing else—I have put in my time.

Self-deceiving as this behavior appears and vain as it has normally proved, few anglers will find it puzzling. Rising trout bring with them the promise of both lofty achievement and primal fulfillment. Consistently ennobled as the most cerebral version of a sport already rarefied by Latin incantations and secret handshakes, fishing the hatch is also the most primitive, the most conducive to sudden elevations in blood pressure, to the twitching of vestigial tailbones, to tripping the hammer on our late-Pleistocene instinct to pounce out there and get one. Hatch fishing exists as one of fly angling's self-evident truths, its own complete explanation.

Harder to account for is why I don't simply overcome my hesitations and relocate to the water farther upriver, where such opportunities arise more predictably. And here I can only gesture lamely toward the kind of irrationality that underlies much of angling—how, for instance, we allege to deepen our appreciation of nature by pestering it, sometimes to death. If fishing were inherently reasonable, you'd probably see a lot more people on the water.

But what anglers do rarely answers to a well-ordered chain of command. Instead, a roundtable of competing impulses jointly negotiates our motives, and so our behavior often exhibits the internally contradictory and self-defeating character of most committee decisions. In this case, I confine myself largely to a ten- or fifteen-mile stretch of this much longer river partly out of an affection born of long association; partly because I know the water well; partly out of expedience—it happens to be nearby and I am somewhat lazy in any number of respects; and partly because I persist in the desire that some secret intersection of place and time—a hatch of one's own—might reveal itself when and where others have not thought to search or have not looked hard enough. It is, let me add, impossible to exaggerate the preposterousness of this fantasy on the Madison, arguably among the most closely scrutinized, thoroughly studied, heavily visited trout streams in North America, water about which virtually everything is known. Nevertheless, I uncork this delusion summer after summer with fresh enthusiasm and a handful of half-baked schemes, nearly all of which have ended in protracted waiting to no point, like a failed police stakeout but without the coffee and doughnuts.

This particular spot where I sit on a stone at the tail of a glassy glide, perspiring in the late August heat, one finger away from sundown, has brought me as close as I've come to finding a private hatch, though its remoteness from a sure thing accurately conveys my pitifully low standards for proximity. I study each little current tongue and the stall of water behind each boulder and the smooth run along the bank, looking from one to the next, searching for signs of flies or fish and frequently checking my watch. Waiting of this sort may look like just killing time, but in fact it boils down to a form of gambling, betting the minutes away, flipping them one by one into the mounting pot, wagering the last of the day against the possibility of caddis and then of trout rising while there's still light enough to fish them. And as in all wagering, the size of the stakes depends upon the alternative value of the currency, how it might otherwise be put to use.

On some evenings, I would take up a position at this spot, resolved to wait regardless of the outcome, only to be worn down by erosive uncertainties as time leaked away. Finally, I'd take a few casts—just poking around the low-percentage water, I'd tell myself, pecking at the edges of the good stuff without disturbing it or alarming the trout I should be lulling into a sense of security; just biding time until the hatch, I'd tell myself, should there even be a hatch, but actually trying, as people will, to have it both ways. Other nights I would rise from the stupor of just sitting there and stumble along the bank from place to place like a man fresh from shock treatment, wondering if fish might be rising somewhere else.

Less than half a mile from this spot, on the far bank, an irrigation ditch snakes along the foot of the bench behind an earthen berm overgrown with foxtail barley and knapweed. It sidles up to the main channel from below, slides the jagged fang of a rock diversion dam beneath the skin of the river, and withdraws an allotment that will reappear from countless brass nozzles on miles of wheel line irrigators that turn a trout stream into water vapor and alfalfa. The dam, however, also deflects the current to my side of the river into a broad and boulder-broken run, too deep and fast to hold much interest for the dry-fly man, but precisely the kind of water that plays crazy brain songs to the plumb-line artist. On some occasions, I would spend time nymphing this stretch while waiting for the hatch, once or twice to profound effect, but never without the troubling thought that I might be missing something, a mounting conviction that the flies would be early tonight, and finally the frantic certainty that they must be hatching at this very moment. I'd charge out of the water and rush upstream, trying to change flies on the run in order to be ready the second I arrived, slowing as I approached the rock garden to check for rises. Then, after five or ten deflating minutes of spotting nothing, I would trudge back down to the nymphing water and force-feed more split shot to the river bottom until the same escalating and unbearable suspicion of trout rising somewhere I wasn't would once again drive me from the water and back upstream to look. I traveled a good bit in those days, looking for a better world.

In short, I once believed it possible, even advisable, to do other things while waiting, though I've since come to see this as a tepid type of commitment with strong overtones of presumptive defeat, like a prenuptial agreement. Still, the liberties open to a man with plenty of time and water all to himself invite the weighing of alternatives, assaying the potential wins and losses of what you have against what you might have chosen. And sitting alongside a river makes such conjectures almost inevitable. Watching all that water coming down from places you aren't fishing, all those possibilities slipping into the past, does make you consider how things could have been different.

One never stops speculating. But traveling back to the theoretical futures that might have been is finally a less telling trip than tracing the single path that accounts for how you arrived at this one particular place and time—all the unforeseen turns, the hazardous crossings, the chance circumstances and random encounters, compasses both faithful and faulty, the fears that you traveled around and the long straight stretches of just going forward, the temporary detours that somehow proved permanent.

Each played a role in the strange logic driving the plot of a life that somehow added up to the unpredicted sum of the moment: sitting on a riverside stone and studying the water, watching for a pot to boil, in wait for the Great Unrevealed that may or may not show up.

"It's not certain," says Vladimir. "No," says Estragon, "nothing is certain." Which is of no great consequence. If I wanted only to catch something, I'd nymph the water downstream, at the least, it's full of whitefish. But there is no significant point to be proved in fishing, unless you wish to demonstrate that you're somehow more clever than the fish, a suspect aspiration to begin with and frequently inconclusive in the end. Nor will catching fish cure what ails you, though I must say it does a commendable job of treating the symptoms. And Norman Maclean notwithstanding, fly fishing is not a religion, for which we may all weep our thanks; at best it can bring you to sacred places and show you a small miracle or two. With that in mind, I have arranged matters to the extent of my capacities. The stage is set. I've taken my spot at the appointed hour, my part memorized, with a small cast of understudies and extras pinned to a foam patch on my vest. The principle players may or may not show up, according to the inscrutable way of things. Waiting for them represents just a distilled and concentrated version of the deep uncertainty that surrounds all fishing—angling, perhaps, in its most abstract form.

The last slanting rays of the sun throw dark pools of shadow behind the hills and long eddies of shade in the lee of bushes and boulders. Never more than in the low, streaming currents of light at sunset does the day resemble moving water. The last of the afternoon heat rises from the earth in faint, sage-scented currents that sweep over you with the feel of raw silk. Crickets test the temperature, find the tempo for the night, and announce the cooling air. The swallows go home and leave the sky to the nighthawks, pivoting pirouettes on the tip of a wing. The deerflies have disappeared, and mosquitoes will remain in the bankside thickets for a while yet. I put on my right wading boot and lace it up snugly, just in case. In the deepening shadows, I take off my sunglasses and let them hang from a cord around my neck, once again caught off guard to find that there's more light left than I'd thought.

Evenings pass quickly this late in the season, with summer poised on the cusp of fall. In half an hour, it will be too dark to see. The river is completely quiet. It doesn't appear that the curtain will rise tonight. Maybe tomorrow.

"Well," asks Estragon, "shall we go?"

"Yes, let's go," says Vladimir.

I consider heading back to the ranch. No doubt some worthwhile merriment or other is being made there, and getting this wading boot off would feel pretty good. But it's too pleasant out here to leave quite yet.

Afterword

As the end of August approaches, the days grow a little shorter and the shadows a little longer; the overnight temperatures dip down to the low forties. The presentiments of fall, perceptible for weeks at higher altitudes, arrive in the valley, and the time comes to quit the ranch. Over the course of several days, people pack up and head off, one or two at a time, and return to other lives. There seems a leave-taking every morning, and afterward, the rest of us regroup and close the spaces, and life at the ranch reshapes itself around this new configuration, though always inside an imaginary triangle formed by the river, the kitchen, and the cottonwoods. These attenuations have less a sense of denouement than of ongoing, scaled-down reconstitutions of community, a continually shifting composition that may vary in its specifics from year to year but never fails to produce its pleasing combinations of people, even as their numbers grow smaller and smaller, until finally only the Painter and I remain. We are invariably the last to leave and frequently stay on for a few days after everyone else has gone, getting the house squared away, drifting the river another time or two, and always concluding the fishing as we began it, spending a day on foot among the islands in the reach of river near town. Then one morning, we load the car, lock the place up, and start for home.

The trip back to Oregon takes fourteen hours and, like all long drives, induces a strange feeling of suspension and disconnectedness. The hours pass differently inside a car, and the numerals on the dashboard clock become increasingly abstract and hypothetical, the time it might be if you were actually somewhere, but meaningless on the road. Arriving back home does little to dispel this impression of dislocated time and much to amplify it. Summer goes by slowly in the more temperate coastal climate here, and everything appears very much unchanged. Just a few signs hint at the weeks that have passed—a touch of red on the apples ripening out back; two or three bushels of accumulated mail; and the grimy, trashed-out vehicle in the driveway. After nearly a straight month's fishing, the outside of my rig looks like the aftermath of a half-successful car bombing; the inside looks like the other half. But beyond this small and unpersuasive evidence, there's little visible confirmation of having ever been away, of time having elapsed at all. The summer we have returned to so seamlessly abuts the summer we left that the interval spent in Montana does not even present itself as a bracketed aside, as parenthetical time slipped unobtrusively into the syntax of ordinary days. Those weeks feel instead detached, clockless and uncalendared, pinched off by the gapless meeting of the place we set out from and the one we returned to.

I am reminded of this again when I run into friends in town who remark that it must have been good to get away and a little hard to return to "real life," though often omitting the quotation marks, as though the existence they refer to is not just another way of construing the world, another kind of performance. Of course I understand what they mean, and there's not much hay to be made in arguing what is "real." The only authenticity of the spaces we fashion lies in the living of them. On the other hand, the Montana I inhabit still suggests a kind of ambiguity. It is, in one respect, a hothouse experience, an artificial habitat of sorts—it is made to be precisely that—and so cannot help but be limited, selective, and unrepresentative, with no authority beyond itself. At the same time, while skimming the cream from a pail of fresh milk may not qualify you as an expert in dairy farming, the cream itself is perfectly authentic and your appreciation of it genuine. There is a version of knowing that comes with extreme locality.

The Montana I have described is a conscious artifice, an invention, imaginary in a sense, though not one that is opposed to "real." The ranch is a created human space inside an existing natural one where living coalesces around landscape and unfolds according to an interior dynamic of its own. It is an improvised narrative, not simply of characters and events but of ritual and memory, of theme and metaphor, of what we choose to make matter. What that narrative is about, exactly, is one of the objects of the narrative to discover. Jointly crafted and made by hand, with everybody's fingerprints all over it, the place, you might say, is a medium of expression, and in this respect bears some resemblance to a work of fiction. Both are containers for the imaginative life within them, spaces deliberately arranged for concentrated experiences that seek not to reproduce but, in some small and local way, to elucidate the world beyond them. Such clarifications are possible in everyday life but seem generally obscured by the labor of livelihood and drowned out by the garble of the world, available only to those who manage to penetrate the static—artists, sometimes, and the abnormally sane. Being neither, I seek out a place that, by nature, gets better reception.

What I have been calling Montana begins in locality, in the raw materials of land and water, and narrative arises as spontaneously and surely from place as it does from character. So intrinsic is the connection, in fact, that it has woven its way almost unnoticed into the language. Franklin Burroughs observes, "The evolution of the word *plot*—first, a patch of land; then, a map of a patch of land; then, a skeleton of a story—seems to be recapitulated in individual experience: what is literal first grows abstract and two-dimensional, then forms itself into a premonition of narrative." And, I would add, sometimes moves beyond premonition to narrative enacted. The word itself did not create this connection but was enlarged in the service of a lived truth, that places and people tell one another's stories.

ACKNOWLEDGMENTS

ACKNOWLEDGING DEBTS IS A POOR SUBSTITUTE FOR SETTLING THEM, BUT for the time being, I hope my thanks will serve as down payment.

I am grateful, once again, to Nick Lyons for his many efforts on behalf of this book; working together has been a pleasure.

Sincerest thanks to Tracy Daugherty and Jim Babb for their insight and indispensable assistance when the manuscript was in draft, and to Bonnie Thompson for her vigilant eye and sharp pencil.

I am immeasurably indebted to Prasad Boradkar, Betty Campbell, Heidi Fisher, Paul Hextell, George Hopper, Cindy Leeson, Greg Leeson, Paul Rothstein, and Jim Schollmeyer, inventors all.

A special thanks to Bill and Betsy Segal for their generosities over the years.

My deepest gratitude to the Painter, for her countless contributions to this book and its making, among a great many other things.